GOD'S ENCOURAGING WORD

From the Books of Wisdom

by

Marvin P. Nail

PRESS

Author's Note

What you will find in these pages are brief meditations on selected passages from the Books of Wisdom (Job through Song of Solomon) in Scripture. They were written as part of my own devotional time to begin each work day. They have served as a means of God's encouragement to me.

When I first began to write these, my goal was to focus on at least one passage from each chapter of the Bible as I came to it. It has been a marvelous journey for me for more than a decade so far and I continue to find the time spent to be a source of great joy to me.

These reflections have not been simply sermonizing devotionals. In each of these meditations I have tried to speak to an important theme of that passage or a larger teaching of Scripture. They do not presume to be more than they are. They have been shared with a growing number of friends over the years who have continued to encourage me to include them in a book to be shared with a wider audience. This is the first of them I submitted for publication.

Many of these meditations have served as a goad to further study and reflection on my own part. They have often led me to a desire for broader development of some of the topics merely touched upon in these. My hope is that they will do the same for you as well.

They have been my gift to myself as well as an offering to God. Their value for you is not mine to assess. That decision will be yours. If they stir you to a deeper study of the Bible for yourself, they will have fulfilled a lifelong goal of mine.

Marvin P. Nail
Nashville, TN
2008

Dedication

This book is dedicated to Nancy, the love of my life, wife of my old age, and my daily inspiration. She has continued to be an avenue of God's blessing to me and has been a major source of His continuing encouragement to me. She fancies herself to be just an ordinary person; but to me that is like saying an early Fall vista in the Smoky Mountains is just a regular autumn day.

But I also wish to dedicate this work to the many who have encouraged me to this point over the many years I have shared some of these thoughts with them. They have led me to believe that a broader audience could find benefit from what God has allowed me to see in His Scriptures.

TABLE OF CONTENTS

JOB

Living with Life's Trials

[He] did not blame God – Job 1:22

How quick we are to want to fix blame when something goes wrong! No matter the problem, we seem to think that if we can ascribe responsibility for the situation we have in some measure solved the problem. Interestingly the blame seldom falls on us. We are almost always able to find some other person at whom we can point the finger. For believers and non-believers the easiest target is God. We too easily blame Him and too seldom give Him credit for the good in our lives. The Scripture teaches us that it is the good in our lives that come from God.

FATHER, teach me to look for the good today and in so doing to be able to see Your hand at work. Amen

_____

He still holds fast his integrity – Job 2:3

We have been told throughout most of our lives that each of us has a price. Each person is said to have a limit beyond which he can no longer withstand temptation. That we are "only human" is an excuse often used for our succumbing to desires at odds with our own best intentions. We claim a weakness which, as believers, we do not have. God gives us the strength to face any kind of temptation. He makes it possible for us to live the life we profess to have in Him.

FATHER, I need Your strength today to hold on to the integrity You have given me in Christ. Amen

---

The small and the great are there – Job 3:19

Throughout history we humans have been in conflict with each other over status within our group. We have seemingly believed that by force or by thought we could prove ourselves superior to some other person. Then having proven this to ourselves we assume the right to dominate others. All of society appears to have become this way. But death has a way of bringing all of humanity to the same level. Then what? Only through our faith is there anything more worthwhile after death.

FATHER, I am thankful that though death is certain, I have the assurance of an eternal life with You. Amen

---

Is not the fear of God your confidence? – Job 4:6

In the latter days of the twentieth century it would be an easy matter to become disillusioned with almost everything. It is certainly a fact that those in leadership in every realm of human endeavor have mostly failed us. We had trusted them to give us direction and to inspire us. They had promised much and delivered so little. Many of them have not only disappointed us but they have made us feel worse about ourselves because we believed in them. But all of mankind will fail us at some point. Our trust in the God of Abraham and the Father of Jesus Christ is our only real hope.

FATHER, when I am tempted to become cynical about the world around me, remind me where my only confidence must lie. Amen

---

Do not despise the discipline of the Almighty
– Job 5:17

One of the mistakes we often make is in equating discipline with punishment. The imposition of punishment on anyone or anything is designed primarily as retribution for unacceptable behavior. Correction or restoration is of only secondary consideration. Discipline, however, has as its priority causing the other to move into a more acceptable behavior. Even God's judgment is aimed at bringing our behavior into line. It becomes punishment only after the discipline is rejected. When we grumble and groan under the pain of God's judgment it is only because we have rejected His correction of our path.

FATHER, Help me to see in the pains of life Your loving hand guiding me into right paths. Amen

---

I have not despised the words of the Holy One
– Job 6:10

Have you ever read anything in the Scriptures that bothered you? If you haven't, you probably need to do more prayerful reading. God's word has a way of exposing to the light of our own understanding the darker side of ourselves that we would often rather not see. When we are discovered by those portion of the Bible that disturb our comfort level we surely do not enjoy it. We may even be angered by some aspects of ourselves that are exposed. But this should lead us to despise our own behavior and not to disparage the word. Believers will sometimes be unsettled by scripture but never to the point of casting it aside.

FATHER, Your words to me are a treasure even though they often ruffle me and disturb my stained spirit. Amen

---

What is man ... that Thou art concerned about him?
– Job 7:17

The psalmist pondered this same question many years later. When you meditate on all the great works of God in creating and sustaining the universe it can cause you to feel very insignificant in the overall scheme of things. This is especially true when you are in the midst of great difficulties. You may be tempted to think that you have somehow gotten lost in the grand shuffle of managing a whole universe. But the good news of the Bible from first page to last is that each member of God's creation is under His watchful eye.

FATHER, my heart is warmed by the knowledge that my life is always within Your care. Amen

———————

He will yet fill your mouth with laughter – Job 8:21

The humor of a situation may be difficult to see when you're in the middle of it. All of us go through times that are so frustrating and unnerving that we can see the circumstance and little else. In our times of sorrow or confusion our hope in God can remain constant. We know that He is bringing good to those who love Him. But in our distress our joy only keeps us steady. The rejoicing comes when we can look back on it with the assurance that God has brought us through.

FATHER, even in today's circumstances, open my heart to rejoice in Your goodness that is on its way because You love me. Amen.

How can a man be in the right before God?
– Job 9:2

We believers spend a lot of our energies striving to be pleasing to God. And well we should. But we have no way of doing enough things to make us right before God. He alone is right. Our striving to please Him is born of our gratitude to Him for what He has done for us in Christ Jesus. We are made acceptable to God only through Jesus. From that love and acceptance we are compelled to serve with all our heart.

FATHER, I will serve You today because I love You. Amen

Thy care has preserved my spirit – Job 10:12

When we face our daily struggles that seem to have no relief in sight, discouragement over such a prospect may increase the burden. The almost inevitable result is that we slide into a miry pit of despair. Hope is shrouded in the gloom of the present. But for the believer this is not the final answer. We know a secret not available to non-believers. We know that our loving Father never leaves us alone. That assurance lifts us out of our dark pit into the light of His presence.

FATHER, I give thanks to You today that You do not allow my disappointments and discouragements to drag me into despair. Amen

---

Can you discover the limits of the Almighty?
– Job 11:7

The psalmist declared that there was no place he might go and be outside the Father's care. In teaching His disciples about faith Jesus declared the awesome power of God open to those who trust Him. To the One who is almighty obviously nothing is beyond His power. But Jesus being allowed to remain on the cross of Calvary and suffer the death of a common criminal for humanity shows something of the limit on God. His own love for us would not let Him stop His own Son's pain and shame by having Him step down from the cross.

FATHER, keep foremost in my mind today the unbridled love You have for me. Amen

---

With Him are strength and sound wisdom
– Job 12:16

Many new and strange voices compete for a hearing in these days. They want to entertain us or inform us. They offer us what we want to hear or at least what they think we want. Even believers who recognize His voice find themselves lured away by the attractive words they hear. These persistent voices pounding in our ears easily drown out the one Voice that has the wisdom and understanding to be of real help to us.

FATHER, help me to be able to sort out the babble and hear Your voice clearly today. Amen

---

Will it be well when He examines you? – Job 13:9

Too many believers assume that when we were converted and had our sins wipes away we no longer had a sin problem. We have been delivered from eternal damnation through the work of Christ. But that should give us no sense of freedom to continue to sin. Can we dare to stand in the loving gaze of our heavenly Father knowing we have failed Him miserably? Because of His overwhelming love are we not compelled to live even more circumspectly for His glory?

FATHER, I bow in amazement in the presence of Your matchless love for me. Amen

---

Who can make the clean out of the unclean?
– Job 14:4

The normal circumstances of life leave stains and scars that man-made cleansers cannot remove. The sins we commit leave an indelible mark on our lives. But the teaching of Scripture and the experience of our own lives tell us that there is a remedy for such stains. Through the work of Jesus Christ on the cross God has provided a means for making us new again and presenting us to Himself without spot or blemish.

FATHER, wash me clean again today from the sins that continue to leave their mark on my life. Amen

---

Are the consolations of God too small for you?
Job 15:11

In times of distress, before we begin to see the hand of God at work, we are often inclined to wonder why He has not come to our aid. When deeply discouraged and feeling alone we may even think for a moment that God is unconcerned about our circumstances. These are the times when we need to recall what God has already done for us. Such recollections will remind us that God does work for us in many small ways, but also that He has proven His love through many enormous acts on our behalf.

FATHER, restrain me from self-pity by the reminder of Your constant care for me. Amen

---

The solace of my lips could lessen your pain
– Job 16:5

Each of us has found ourselves at a loss for words in critical times. We have wanted so desperately to be able to comfort a friend in sorrow or distress but the words that did come to mind sounded so empty and powerless when they came from our mouth. In such times we have wanted to give help and encouragement but have felt so inadequate. For those times a silent presence spoke with more eloquence than rivers of spoken words.

FATHER, make my spoken and written words always helpful and my silent presence uplifting. Amen

---

Nevertheless the righteous shall hold to his way
– Job 17:9

The world around us is constantly putting pressure on us to compromise our faith. Some of the temptations seem innocent and insignificant enough at first glance. Some of them are so powerful that we begin to believe that we simply cannot help ourselves (which is true, by the way). We readily yield to some of these, telling ourselves that "we're only human." But persons of faith need not be overcome by the lure of any temptation. We do not overcome by OUR strength, but by the might of the One who dwells within us.

FATHER, remind me today that when I am tempted it is Your strength that enables me to have the victory. Amen

---

Show understanding and then we can talk
– Job 18:2

How often we find ourselves talking to someone and it seems like we're talking to a wall! The problem most of the time is that the other person has his/her own agenda. For communication to take place both parties must make an effort to hear each other. That usually means we must lay aside our own agenda to make sure we hear what the other person is trying to tell us. When they have been heard they are usually more apt to listen to us.

FATHER, teach me to hear first so that I may then speak with greater wisdom. Amen

---

I know that my Redeemer lives – Job 19:25

From time to time we hear of the death of some person known to many around our nation or the world. Because of the impact they had in life they will be remembered of a long time. But they are still dead. All we will ever gain have of them is memory. Many heroes fill the pages of history books and are remembered for their great deeds in bygone days. Yet they too are dead. But the Man who died centuries ago and is remembered and revered most to this day is not dead at all. He is very much alive and well and coming soon to take us to His home.

FATHER, remind me today that my faith is not in a memory but in a hope that is steadfast and sure. Amen

---

The joy of the godless [is] momentary – Job 20:5

Many of us wonder at times at the prosperity and overall good times the unsaved seem to have in life. Everything appears to be going their way while God does not give us blessings like that. Some believers are even prone to envy the charmed lives the unsaved seem to lead. But we should know better. The lost may have many of the things of this world; however, this world is about to end along with all its things. As believers we have treasures stored up in heaven where we will live eternally with Jesus. Tell me, who's richer?

FATHER, though I live in a world of things, guard me from becoming too attached to them. Amen

---

The wicked is reserved for the day of calamity
– Job 21:30

One of the greatest blessings of becoming a child of God through faith in the work of Jesus Christ is that we have a home reserved in heaven for all eternity. We love to sing about that and listen to preachers speculate about when we will be going to that fair land. For some perverse reason we also like to hear them talk about the damnation of the lost. It's almost as though we want them to get what's coming to them. Our joy should rather be in the hope that hell's confines would be empty of all but the devil and his minions.

FATHER, burden my heart with the lost among those I know until their reservation in hell is canceled. Amen

———————————

The Almighty will be your gold and choice silver to
you – Job 22:25

Almost everyone desires security for them-selves now ans in their golden years. We like certainty and become settles when circumstances disrupt our plans and goals in life. But we must not allow ourselves to become obsessed with physical and financial security. Such aims can cripple us in the service of God. Launching out in faith is not possible if we are unwilling to release our grip on our things trusting that the Lord really is sufficient for us.

FATHER, help me not to hold so tightly to my things that my heart and life are not open to You. Amen

---

I have kept His way and not turned aside
– Job 23:11

Most people I have known would not hesitate to say that they are good people. And they are. They have not committed any heinous crime and they are law-abiding. They have basically been true to the laws of God. But to say that they have always stayed on the right path without an occasional misstep is beyond even the best. Why do we all insist on taking those brief side trips into the dark alleys of sin? Why would we want to leave the heavenward road even for a moment in the outskirts of hell?

FATHER, give me strength and wisdom to keep my feet from straying from Your path today. Amen

---

His eyes are on their ways – Job 24:23

Knowing that someone is looking over your shoulder while you work or is watching your every move from a distance can be unnerving. It can also cause your adrenaline to increase so that you can perform above your normal limits. The knowledge that the eyes of God are on us can bother us if we are contemplating sin. However, when we are secure in the knowledge that we are living under the watchful eye of a loving Father we can live truly free.

FATHER, I rejoice today in the knowledge that Your loving eyes are watching over me. Amen

---

How then can a man be just with God? – Job 25:4

This has been the question of humankind sense the dawn of time when the creature first recognized the presence of the Creator. Countless methods have been employed with every kind of understanding about who or what the Creator was and is. Even today among people who acknowledge who the Creator is there exists a wide variety of attempts to get right with God. Some seek merit through achievement, others through self-denial, and still others think they don't have to bother. But God has declared that the only Way to reconciliation is through the work of Jesus Christ.

FATHER, remind me today that my relationship with You has been established and is maintained through Jesus. Amen

---

Behold, these are the fringes of His ways
– Job 26:14

We strive to be aware of what God is doing in the world around us. We often look for some spectacular event to signal the hand of God. As a consequence we usually overlook God at work in the small things that are so vital to our welfare. But, large or small, we only see a fraction of the work of God. His full glory is such that we are not able to comprehend it. His works are so wonderful and so mighty that we cannot bear the enormity of it all. We content ourselves with less awareness because we are more comfortable with it.

FATHER, I am overwhelmed with the thought that in all Your majesty and power You should still care for such as me. Amen

---

My lips certainly will not speak unjustly – Job 27:4

Gossip is a practice most of us despise, but which most of us practice from time to time. Many of us have felt the hurtful effects of words spoken in anger or out of jealousy or pettiness. Even knowing that pain we still engage in those sort of words ourselves. But we like to characterize our words differently. The spoken word has tremendous power and must be used by believers to build up and not tear down. We must keep a tight rein on our tongue and evaluate our words before they are uttered lest they cause injury to another.

FATHER, may the words of my mouth and even the thoughts in my heart be acceptable to You today. Amen

---

To depart from evil is understanding – Job 28:28

Resisting temptation is always a tough job. If the decision is not difficult then there is no real temptation. While we are accustomed to prayer and seeking the face of God the resisting is made somewhat easier because of the presence of the power of God in our life. By the same token resisting is always made more difficult when we permit ourselves to linger near the temptation. The best course of action is to remove yourself even from the vicinity of the troubler.

FATHER, because You know my weaknesses, give me wisdom to leave the scene of my potential sin against You. Amen

---

By His light I walked through darkness – Job 29:3

Each day we travel over territory we've not seen before. Even in the sameness of a routine job we daily discover new twists and unexpected turns. Stumbling blindly through life seems to be the fate of all creatures on this planet. However, for the child of God there is help and hope. We do not make the journey alone. Our heavenly Father assures us of His companionship and He not only knows the way, He IS the Way. Even the deepest darkness does not cause Him to stumble and it is He who holds our hand.

FATHER, give me courage even in the darkest of times knowing that even the darkness is light to You. Amen

---

My prosperity has passed away like a cloud
– Job 30:15

We are reminded every day of the good sense of preparing ourselves financially for the latter years of our life. Many, if not most, of us spend a lot of our time getting our material goods into such a position that we can withstand some of the adverse circumstances that may arise. But we should understand that no material possession is beyond the reach of adversity. What a wonderful idea it would be for us to spend at least as much time preparing ourselves spiritually for those seemingly inevitable downturns in life.

FATHER, remind me to continually seek a closer relationship with You so that all these other concerns will fall into their proper place. Amen

---

Does He not see my ways, and number all my steps?
– Job 31:4

In a society where the majority has become a faceless number or statistic, it is easy to get the feeling you are unimportant, that your life and/or death would have little meaning to the world around you, it is increasingly essential to survival to know that your life and your death matter. The struggle for survival would be pointless if it had no significance to anyone. The message of the gospel is that you and I DO matter to God and that He does SO LOVE you and me.

FATHER, I thank You today that my every step is of great importance to You. Amen

---

He justified himself before God – Job 32:2

None of us likes to be accused of wrongdoing. When we are, we rush to our own defense apparently out of fear that no one else will do so. Even when we begin to feel the pangs of regret because of our sin we hurry to excuse ourselves in an attempt to soothe the anguish of guilt. But when we attempt to justify ourselves we make ourselves a god. Only our heavenly Father can make us right because only He can forgive the sin and "cleanse us from all unrighteousness."

FATHER, I long to be cleansed and made right with You today. Amen

---

He has redeemed my soul from going to the pit
– Job 33:28

Have you ever been in "the pit," the "slough of despond," the pit of despair? Many of us have

31

visited places like that in our life. The stopover may have been caused by great sorrow, disappointment, discouragement, or even stress. The time of our stay might have been a few minutes or many days. But, as a child of God we have also known the joy of being lifted from the miry clay by the strong and loving arm of our heavenly Father. We may climb into the pit but our Lord does not leave us there.

FATHER, I thank You that Your care lifts me from the pits of circumstance as well as the deep holes of my own making. Amen

---

If I have done iniquity I will do it no more
– Job 34:32

The Bible does not hesitate to remind us that all of us have sinned against God. Our decision at this point is how we will respond to this fact. Many seem to have the idea that they might as well keep on sinning. Others, tragically, think that because of their sin they are beyond help or hope. Our heavenly Father encourages us in His word to turn from our wicked ways so that He can forgive and heal us. And yet, far too many of God's children continue to dabble in sin ignoring the coming death of their witness.

FATHER, give me the victory today over the sins that linger in the shadows of my daily walk. Amen

---

God will not listen to an empty cry – Job 35:13

Like small children manipulating adults, we are not beyond trying to manipulate God. Our prayers sometimes are little different from some magical incantations designed to persuade God to do what we want. We carefully choose words we think will cause Him to see our petition as legitimate and somehow worthy of granting. We apparently fail to see prayer for what it really is, the open communication between two who are on such intimate terms that words are almost unnecessary and to whom superficial chatter is an insult.

FATHER, because You know my heart help me not to waste our intimate times together. Amen

---

Do not long for the night – Job 36:20

Night is often thought of as a time for evil activities. It is well-suited for nefarious activities because they are most easily hidden. However, night is not necessary for evil. Many of us only need a time or place where those we know will not be aware of what we are doing. But we cannot find a place so dark or so isolated from the view of others that we can escape the gaze of God. One of the keys to victory over temptation is the understanding that all our activities are within full view of the One before whom we will stand in judgment.

FATHER, remind me that my life is lived under Your watchful eyes and that this fact should cause me to rejoice. Amen

---

That all men may know His work – Job 37:7

Why are we on this earth? That is a question often asked by young people seeking to find their niche in life. Increasingly it is being asked by persons in mid-life who feel that they have lost their way or for whom earlier goals in life now seem less worthy. Some older believers have wondered why God has not yet taken to their eternal home. The answer to these questions for believers can best be seen as our continuing ministry to a world that does not yet trust in Him.

FATHER, I yield myself to You today to show forth Your work in my part of the world. Amen

---

Have you ever in your life commanded the morning? – Job 38:12

To the arrogant, self-made women or men, who survey the world around themselves and take credit to themselves for all the good they see, this is an humbling word from God. To the rebellious and unconcerned persons who want nothing to do with the divine, this is a warning word from God. To the discouraged and despairing persons who feel deserted and alone, this is a comforting and encouraging word from God who is also your loving Father and Creator of the ends of the universe.

FATHER, remind me again today that it is in Your hand that my life rests each moment of the day. Amen

---

He laughs at fear and is not dismayed – Job 39:22

This is the picture of one in the service of a powerful master. We do spend too much of our time and energy worrying about the consequences of being obedient to our Master and Lord Jesus Christ. He tells us from the beginning that a decision to be His servant will not mean a life of comfort and peace in this world. But He also tells us that He Himself is our Comforter and our Peace and that with Him is all power. What need do we have then for fear?

FATHER, give me the willingness to serve You with abandon today. Amen

---

What can I reply to Thee? – Job 40:4

Many of us, having been caught in some wrong-doing, immediately begin inventing excuses for our behavior. We learn this at an early age. Our culture has been influenced by certain schools of psychology to appeal to environment and other circumstances beyond our control to explain why we do what we do. The bottom line is as the Scripture says, we are without excuse before God. He has provided all we need to live as He commands. And He has provided all we need to live with joy.

FATHER, help me to submit to Your love and care so that I need make no excuse. Amen

---

Who has given to Me that I should repay him?
– Job 41:11

Sometimes we act as though God is obligated to do certain things for us. This may be the childish notion that we should always get everything we want. Or it may be the arrogance of adulthood that believes we have earned the things we want from life. But the Bible tells us that the only thing we have really earned or deserve to receive from God is death. But God has obligated Himself to more toward us. He has imposed upon Himself the duty of love.

FATHER, among all the things I might ask of You, the one thing that fulfills all my needs is Your love for me. Amen

---

I have declared that which I did not understand
– Job 42:3

How arrogant of us to think even for a moment that we comprehend God or the things of God! Our theologies and dogmatics are at best merely out-of-focus observations. We can look out from our secure places of contemplation and make broad pronouncements about the Omnipotent One. Afterwards God sometimes blesses us with a lonely walk in the paths of experience where real theology originates. Then we are able to see with more clarity and come to true understandings of God and His care for us.

FATHER, help me to trust You even when I cannot see so that what I do see will be made clearer for me. Amen

---

PSALMS

The Songbook of Faith

His delight is in law of the Lord — Psa. 1:2

That which brings us pleasure in life is usually thought of as family, a hobby, a special relationship or some other such good thing. These are the activities to which we turn for encouragement, to lift our self-esteem, or just simply to relax from the stress of our daily routine. Does it ever occur to us that all of these needs are more than met by spending time in the Scriptures? The great saints of God have always been able to find that refreshment in the Word.

FATHER, I do delight in Your word and thank You for the refreshment that it always brings to my heart. Amen

Worship the Lord ... and rejoice with trembling
— Psa. 2:11

We have in this part of the twentieth century become such pals with God that we have lost much of the sense of wonder at His infinity. We speak of His power and His love and His holiness as though we fully understand those divine traits. We seldom stand in awe of God any longer. But whatever terms we may use to describe God they are woefully inadequate. In His presence we have reason to tremble, not out of fright but in awe and anticipation of what He is doing among us.

FATHER, though I long to behold You in fullness, I shudder at what I have already seen of Your grace toward a sinner like me. Amen

---

I awoke, for the Lord sustains me — Psa. 3:5

So much of life is routine that we often lose sight of the wonder of it all. We give little thought to the complex processes of life that enable us to do the simplest of things. Who among us considers the conglomeration of operations required to walk across a room, or to read the newspaper? When we close our eyes to sleep so that our body may be refreshed, think of all the body activity that continues so that we can awake again. And our heavenly Father's watchful eye keeps account of all these operations in all of us.

FATHER, may my waking thought always be a thanksgiving for Your loving care. Amen

———————

Thou hast put gladness in my heart — Psa. 4:7

Surely this must be the testimony of every child of God! Though your stand for your faith may have brought you animosity from others or even brought you some measure of persecution, you have also known a joy deep within that did not fade. The reason such gladness is possible is that you know and are able to see that God is working for your good. He has even given us a vision of the glory that will one day come to pass. Why should we let our hearts be downcast?

FATHER, in the midst of the gloom that may come my way today, remind me that the source of my highest joy is always in You. Amen

———————

By Thine abundant lovingkindness I will enter Thy house — Psa. 5:7

Going to church can easily become a meaningless ritual with little or no benefit. We make it this way by our own expectations. When we analyze the worth of our time at church in terms of our rating of the music or the sermon we are apt to receive much reward for our visit to the holy place. However, if we will remember that it is by the mercy of God that we have been redeemed and by that same mercy that we are allowed into His presence, then we can be assured that whatever anyone else may do there we will have had a meaningful time in God's house.

FATHER, I am grateful today that wherever I am I can be in Your house as long as my heart is open to You.

The Lord receives my prayer — Psa. 6:9

All of us have gone through those times in our spiritual life when it seemed that the heavens were as brass and our prayers were not reaching the Almighty. The only time we seem to feel that way is when the circumstances of our life are going awry. But more especially in the dark hours the open ear of God is of utmost importance. If in the time of our deepest hurt we feel that the heavenly Father is not listening we are without hope. But thanks be to God it is in just such times that we can have confidence that He see, He hears, and He cares.

FATHER, thank You for the assurance that You are more attentive to my prayer than a mother is to the whimper of a child. Amen

---

The righteous God tries the hearts and minds
— Psa. 7:9

Day after day we live under the critical eye of those around us who may not know us at all. Yet their judgment of us may have a devastating impact on our family and our career. For that reason we learn how to create the right image in the eyes of those who are watching us. Thankfully, and perhaps woefully, our Father does not judge us by superficial means. He is not misled or impressed so much by outward appearances. He knows our hearts and minds and holds us accountable on that level.

FATHER, may the meditations of my heart be pleasing to You today. Amen

---

What is man, that Thou dost take thought of him?
— Psa. 8:4

Only a few of us mortals hold ourselves in very high esteem. Even if we do have a healthy self regard we are usually surprised when the opinions of others are also positive ones. Most of us do not have an accurate estimation of our value, but then we are not in position to do that. The awesome fact is that in the vast span of God's creative work, He chose humankind as the object of His greatest affection. Perhaps even more staggering is the fact that in spite of our sin He should care enough to give the greatest sacrifice for us.

FATHER, I will live today with great joy because I am in Your mind. Amen

---

He does not forget the cry of the afflicted
— Psa. 9:12

Despite the adage to the contrary, misery cannot enjoy company because it has none. There is a loneliness brought on by suffering that is unique to that sufferer. Attempts at sympathy usually fall short of real comfort because they come from the safe distance of not understanding. Only one who is willing to share our suffering or sorrow can break through the barrier of alone-ness. The One who can do this is our heavenly Father. His presence causes any circumstance of life to be elevated to a new level where joy and peace are possible.

FATHER, in my times of distress today remind me of Your presence and care. Amen

---

Why has the wicked spurned God? — Psa. 10:13

Most persons who have not known relationship with Christ have no real reason for rejecting Him. Usually it is a matter of giving it little thought. Before we meet Christ we seldom are in open hostility. But those of us who have trusted Christ look back and wonder why we wasted even a single day of life apart from Him. Now we are moved to wonder how anyone could fail to trust Him. It may be that no one has as yet asked them to trust Him. Maybe now we may be moved to ask.

FATHER, help me to be open today to give a word of witness to someone who may not know you as Lord and Savior. Amen

---

The upright will behold His face — Psa. 11:7

Entering the presence of a ruler has always been a privilege reserved for a select group. Some manage such an audience by extraordinary achievement or service. Others are given access because they helped the ruler get his position. But a member of that ruler's family can go in and out at will. As believers we are children of the King of kings. He has granted access to His throne room because of His love for us.

FATHER, even when You are displeased with Me I will seek Your face because there my sin is wiped away. Amen

---

I will set him in the safety for which he longs
— Psa. 12:5

Our culture is obsessed with security. We demand that all the products we purchase be devoid of any dangers. We expect our parents to protect us when we are young and the government to protect us when we are older. We insist that someone remove all the sharp edges fro life. We devour every news item, magazine, or book that purports to reveal new ways of protecting ourselves and insuring long and healthy life. But only God can give us the security we seek. He alone has the power and permanence to provide the safety we need.

FATHER, thank You for providing eternal life with You which is my only real security. Amen

---

Because He has dealt bountifully with me
— Psa. 13:6

Is this not the testimony of every child of God? Though each of us has walked through valleys and shadows, for they are part of the very fabric of life, we have discovered perhaps only at the end that we were not alone in our journey. He has made our most grievous burden bearable. He has made our highest joy possible. Indeed, He has not dealt with me according to my sin but according to His great mercy.

FATHER, because of Your outrageous goodness to me I offer You my all today. Amen

---

God is with the righteous generation — Psa. 14:5

In this crowded, hectic age it is still not uncommon even for a believer to feel alone. Many of the circumstances of daily living isolate us from each other and sometimes even from God. But God does not leave us to ourselves. The isolation we feel is self-imposed. Though we are certain that those around us do not understand us and what we are going through we can be assured that God does understand and He is with us.

FATHER, I thank You for Your presence with me today. Amen

He ... speaks truth in his heart — Psa. 15:2

Some of us live our lives out of touch with reality. Even our faith is, in large measure, fantasy. We force ourselves to give assent to doctrines we can't make ourselves believe. We seem to want to coerce our minds into accepting these ideas apparently because we believe that is what faith is. But real faith is based on a revelation of truth that has confronted the heart. This undeniable truth allows us to live with a new perspective from which our response to life need not be a facade of belief.

FATHER, thank You for making it possible for me to live from my heart and be true to You. Amen

---

I have no good besides Thee — Psa. 16:2

Many of us, on our way into adulthood, simply must try alternatives. We are compelled by that stage of maturity to challenge our parents' value system, religion, and authority of every kind. During that unsettled period many would-be guides come along to show us better ways of achieving the good life. We are willing to experiment with these options in our quest for the best kind of life. Only after these efforts can some of us see for ourselves that our search was all in vain. Only then are we able to surrender to the One who is the definition of what is good.

FATHER, remind me that my only real option in life is You. Amen

---

I have called upon Thee, for Thou wilt answer — Psa. 17:6

We humans like to solve our own problems. From the earliest years of our lives we assert our independence. We may not be capable of doing everything alone but we do want to give that a try first. When all else has failed we turn to another for assistance. We resort to those who have proven to be able and willing. Believers do not hesitate to go to the Father in time of need because we are confident that He is more than adequate for our need and desires to help us because of His great love.

FATHER, remind me in my times of weakness that You are the source of strength for me. Amen

---

He brought me forth ... into a broad place
— Psa. 18:19

The pressures of daily life in today's world is simply overwhelming to many. Deadlines on the job, due dates for bills, worries about future expenses, or the future of your current job are among the concerns that cause some to throw up their hands in resignation. Whatever may have us feeling hemmed in can destroy our lives. As believers we may look to God for relief from these burdens. But He does not take the problems away. He relieves the pressure by increasing our strength and by giving us a different perspective of these troubling matters.

FATHER, I thank You for broadening my vision so that I can understand the broad way You have set before me. Amen

---

There is no speech, nor are there words — Psa. 19:3

Our age is characterized by a profusion of words both written and spoken. We admire persons who are able to find the precise word to describe what they have seen or have thought. Believers especially honor those who are able to put into words a systematic description of God in all His attributes. And yet in our hearts we know that we understand so little about God. We have come to understand that even God could not put Himself into words we could understand, so He sent the Word to become one of us so we could see.

FATHER, help me to be in the flesh today a picture of You that someone needs to see. Amen

---

Now I know that the Lord saves — Psa. 20:6

Perhaps you have been through some of those dark valleys that seem to have no end. Our minds imagine the worst of dangers lurking in the shadows. Fear grips us with such power that all of life seems caught up in it and strangled by it. But for the believer there comes a light not always seen with the eye. Rather it is a Light known only through faith. That light is the hope we have because of Jesus Christ. That hope is the assurance that our Lord delivers and will deliver us in our hour of need.

FATHER, remind me of Your continuing work of salvation so that I may be empowered to serve You with my whole heart today. Amen

---

Thou dost meet him with the blessings of good things — Psa. 21:3

Each day for a believer is conceived in the heart of God for the good of His children. His days dawn in love from the heavenly Father who has hidden undeserved blessings just around each bend in the day's path. Those days march along through some shadowy places where His care is often the only light. His companionship brings us to the close of each day with joy. And His grace brings us to our bed of rest each night with the assurance that we will wake in His love again tomorrow.

FATHER, thank You for the blessing I always find when I come into Your presence even by accident on my part. Amen

---

They trusted, and Thou didst deliver them
— Psa. 22:4

What can we do to receive eternal life? This has been the question asked by religious and non-religious persons throughout the ages. Mankind has devised many solutions to this dilemma. Various religious systems have offered their own prescriptions for immortality. The Scriptures offer a simple solution to the problem. The Bible says that eternal life belongs to whoever is willing to trust God. It is the trusting ones who are being delivered and brought into eternity with the Father.

FATHER, I trust You today and ask that You help me to trust You more. Amen

---

He restores my soul — Psa. 23:3

Everyone gets tired from play or work or even doing nothing. This is not all bad. Our body needs to exert itself so that its muscles may continue to develop and maintain their usefulness. However, the body does need a time for rest and renewal. Many of us in these days also get spiritually tired. This happens when we are doing too many religious things. We are so busy with our church activities that our spirits are drained of vital energy and some suffer burn out. Each of us needs that quiet time with God to get our spiritual "second wind" so that we may be of greater service to our Lord.

FATHER, thank You for these moments I am able to have with You each day. Amen

---

He shall receive a blessing from the Lord
— Psa. 24:5

Much of our society today is concerned with their rights or their entitlements. This is especially true in our relationships with government or even other people. But our relationship with God is different. Getting what we deserved is not what we want from Him. When we lean upon His mercy, however, we can always expect good things from His loving hand. He has promised to shower us with His blessings each day. That promise always gives us something good in our future.

FATHER, thank You for the ways You have already planned to bless me today. Amen

---

For Thee I wait all the day — Psa. 25:5

None of us cares much for having to wait. We get frustrated and sometimes give up or go off on our own. Waiting on God is, for some, just as annoying. But we are not like the pagans who must go through all the right motions and hope that by so doing they have pleased their gods and earned his/her favor. Rather we are more like the young child waiting for a parent to get home from work so that they can do something together. The waiting does not bring frustration. Instead it increases anticipation so that when our Father comes to us we fairly explode with joy.

FATHER, though I know You are always present with me, I long to be at work with You today. Amen

---

I have trusted in the Lord without wavering
— Psa. 26:1

Like sheep, wandering seems to be a part of our nature. It's not that we have trouble focusing. The trouble comes because our focus, again like sheep, is on immediate gratification of need. We think far less about who or what meets our perceived need. We simply want what we want when we want it. If God does not supply what we want quickly it is all too easy for us to seek another supplier. But our heavenly Father still seeks those who will be faith-full, trusting Him no matter what because He will supply all our needs by Christ Jesus.

FATHER, remind me today that You are my only need. Amen

In spite of this I shall be confident — Psa. 27:3

Taking life "one day at a time" is a popular prescription in these days. But taken one day at a time one could come close to losing faith in God. Each day may have sufficient difficulties that could make us think God does not care, if we only looked at that day. But as believers we are encouraged to look not just at one day but at all the days that lie ahead. In spite of what may happen in our life today we have the assurance that all our days are in God's hand. We can know that this one day is not all there is to our life with God.

FATHER, help me to put today and its problems in the perspective that all of my life is in Your loving care. Amen

---

With my song I shall thank Him — Psa. 28:7

Many religions are characterized by somberness or fear in their worship or appeasement of their deities. The worship of the God of Abraham, Isaac, and Jacob, the Father of our Lord Jesus Christ, has always begun with song. From earliest times songs have been the method of expression of joy and thankfulness. What better way for our hearts to burst forth with thanksgiving than in song? The joy engendered by the mercy and grace of God through Jesus cannot be constricted into solemn meditation. Such exuberance gratefully has an adequate outlet in song.

FATHER, because You are the source of my highest joy I lift my song to You today. Amen

---

In His temple everything says, "Glory!"
— Psa. 29:9

Like Jesus dealing with the people using the temple as part of their money-making scheme, most of us would be opposed to use of the church for activities totally unrelated to the Christian gospel. However, many of us would think that some of the events at church are at best marginally related to the gospel. We do need to take care that the church facilities remain tied to our message. But a far more serious problem is associated with our convenient memory lapse in relation to our bodies being temples of God. Does our body give appropriate glory to God?

FATHER, help me to hold this dwelling place of Your Spirit as a sacred temple to give glory to Your name. Amen

---

His anger is but for a moment, His favor is for a lifetime — Psa. 30:5

We lowly humans know so little about forgiveness. We are able to cool our anger but we seldom are able to get rid of ill feelings toward one who has wronged us. Not so with God. Sin always stirs the wrath of God because of what it does to His children. But when God forgives, He also forgets. This does not mean that He loses His memory, but that He no longer holds the wrong against us. God's matchless grace is such that He can bestow His favor on the vilest sinner who repents and trusts in Him.

FATHER, lift my spirit today with the reminder of Your unending grace. Amen

---

I am like a broken vessel — Psa. 31:12

Each of us has at some time in our life come to the point of despair. Perhaps it was because our circumstances were such that we felt outdone by them and at our wits end. Perhaps it was because we had come under conviction for the sin in our life and were overwhelmed by the sense of separation from God. In those times we feel broken and hopeless and useless. But then the Potter comes to us and gathers up all the fragments of our life in His mercy. In His grace He then puts them together into a vessel that honors Him and is honored by Him.

Father, again today I hand You some pieces of my life that I have broken off so that You can make me whole yet again. Amen

---

Blessed is the man in whose spirit is no guile
— Psa. 32:2

We learn from earliest days how to manipulate and mislead others. We begin to be less trusting of others because we know our own hearts and know that we are less open and honest. We have difficulty not being suspicious of words and motives in others for the same reason. When we meet a person like the one described in our text, it is difficult to believe he is not just skillful in masking his real nature. One way each of us can become more like this blessed person is to live like one with nothing to hide.

Father, help me to live today so that I will be unashamed to have my life open to all. Amen

---

A warrior is not delivered by great strength
— Psa. 33:16

Each of us has his/her heroes. We always seem to need someone to inspire us. We admire and even emulate those who appear successful. Even in religious matters we are anxious to know how they achieved their status so that we can copy their method or program and be successful too. But true spiritual heroes deny that status. Instead of drawing attention to themselves, like panes of glass they let us see what's on the other side.

FATHER, should anyone look to me today may they see You through my life. Amen

_____

His praise shall continually be in my mouth
— Psa. 34:1

Few people have a problem being thankful when someone does them a favor. And even fewer can suppress gratitude when good comes from a person whom we have mistreated. Is it any wonder then that we should find it easy to be thankful to God? He has been faithful with goodness toward us even when we were unfaithful to Him. God has always brought good to His creation. We never fail to have reason to give Him praise.

FATHER, remind me today of many of Your expressions of goodness so that I may be driven again to break forth in praise. Amen

_____

When they were sick, my clothing was sackcloth
— Psa. 35:13

Many of us are willing to pray for someone who is sick or in some other distress. But often our praying is little more than recitations of someone's troubles to a God who already knows anyway. Most pray-ers are accustomed to "take your burdens to the Lord and leave them there." But too often we take names and conditions to the Lord without ever first taking them on as a burden of compassion. Real prayer does not eliminate caring to the point of feeling the hurts of others.

FATHER, help me to share the pain of those around me so that my praying may come from a heart of compassion. Amen

---

With Thee is the fountain of life — Psa. 36:9

At various times in our lives we seek out a source of spiritual water that will slake our thirst. In those searches we almost always begin by stopping at the many readily available puddles of stagnant water the world has to offer us. If there were no other place to find water these would have to do. But always within our reach are the freely flowing fountains of God's refreshing water of life. Until we taste of this fountain nothing can satisfy. Having tasted these waters we will never thirst again.

FATHER, quench my thirst for You again today. Amen

Trust in the Lord, and do good — Psa. 37:3

The first and greatest obstacle to salvation is not our sin but our willingness to trust. Living in this world quickly hammers trust from your system as you learn that almost nothing or no one is trustworthy. But believers, having overcome that barrier to salvation, have another obstacle. This is not an obstacle to salvation but a hindrance to the joy. A life of service is the purpose of the life in Christ. Our heavenly Father gave us new life in Christ so that we could spend that life doing good in His name. There is the true joy of this salvation found.

FATHER, use me to do good for at least one person today. Amen

----

I am full of anxiety because of my sin — Psa. 38:18

Most of us have never thought of our sin as being very bad. We have not been murderers, adulterers or thieves. We tend to think of our sins as more like mistakes or misdemeanors. The truth of the matter is that the penalty for sin is separation from God and the only remedy for that sin is the sacrifice made by Jesus of Nazareth. It is surely a painful thing to recall the enormity of the consequences of our sin. But we need to be reminded of it so that we can more fully understand the breadth and height and depth of the love of God toward us.

FATHER, remind me that You would have gone to the same extreme if it had only been me in need of salvation. Amen

---

Let me know how transient I am — Psa. 39:4

Our mortality is not a worthy topic of discussion or even pondering to most of us. Even though we know that death will come, it is still a subject we would prefer not to think about. Though we are aware that death can strike at any moment, most of us have convinced ourselves that we will live a long and happy life. But the assumption of long life causes too many of us to postpone dealing with spiritual matters. The Scriptures remind us just how uncertain continued physical life is. It would serve us better if we kept in mind have fragile our physical existence is so that we could give more value to what we have now and what will be ours in eternity.

FATHER, remind me of my approaching death so that I may treat each new day with awe. Amen

---

*Thou, O Lord, wilt not withhold Thy compassion
from me — Psa. 40:11*

Throughout the history of humanity gods have been seen as basically hostile to mankind. Their favor was something to be courted and achieved only after a variety of efforts to appease them. The God of Abraham was often seen in the same way. But the coming of Jesus put the character in a whole new light for many. The child born in Bethlehem revealed a God who cared so much for His creatures that He was willing to put Himself on the line. Such a God demonstrates a compassion beyond our comprehension but always close at hand.

FATHER, in my moments of self-pity today remind me of Your constant care for me. Amen

---

*Blessed is he who considers the helpless
— Psa. 41:1*

Ours is a selfish age. We can get emotional and even dole out some cash for poor and hungry children half a world away; but we seem to have far less concern for the needs under our noses. It is as though we assume someone else will take care of them, maybe even the government. We seem to forget that the ministry of Jesus was most characterized by His helping the helpless and hopeless. If we would be like Jesus those in need would be high on our list of priorities. In fact, He taught us that giving assistance to such people was a service to Him.

FATHER, open my eyes and my heart to those in need around me today. Amen

---

Hope in God, for I shall yet praise Him
— Psa. 42:11

Almost all of us are prisoners to schedules of some sort. We may like to be early, try to be on time, and many of us constantly worry about being late. We hold others to at least as rigid a standard often becoming irritated when others are late. We sometimes try to put God on schedule too. We decide when we want Him to intervene and when He doesn't meet our schedule for Him we become upset and may even have a crisis of faith. But God is not on our time schedule or else we would be God. However, our only hope is still in God and He has never disappointed one of His children.

FATHER, remind me again today to keep my hope in You because You are the only reason for praise. Amen

---

I will go to . . . God my exceeding joy — Psa. 43:4

In time of sorrow each of us seeks out those who will not just commiserate with us but who will lift us up. In times of happiness or excitement we seek out someone who will not just be happy with us but who will in the sharing make our joy more complete. You have surely learned by now that the One who always restores our joy and even increases it is the same One who brought us joy in the beginning. He is the One who through the anguish of Jesus has made possible a joy unspeakable that endures in spite of circumstances.

FATHER, I rejoice today in the knowledge of Your promised presence with me. Amen

---

Our steps have not deviated from Thy way
— Psa. 44:18

We are taught from our earliest days as believers to constantly beat our breasts and declare our unworthiness of the grace of God. Such self-deprecation is considered a sign of real spirituality. But when our emphasis is constantly on our weaknesses we all too easily make ourselves still weaker and begin to assume failure in any endeavor. An awareness of our strengths would be of more benefit to us as we seek to be of service to God. Even more power and confidence would come as we realize that the One who has all power and authority in heaven and earth is with us. Then a life of purity and obedience would be possible to us.

FATHER, remind me today that my bent toward sinning is no longer Your desire for me nor is it inevitable since I have been redeemed. Amen

---

I will cause Thy name to be remembered
— Psa. 45:17

Think for a moment about when and how you remember first learning about Jesus. It may have been in your home or at your church. Perhaps it was a friend who first told you about Him. Now think for another moment about how many people will be able to say that they learned about Him from you. Once we have come to know Jesus as our personal Savior we have no higher purpose in life than to see that others know Him too. How else will they ever know His salvation?

FATHER, may my words and my life be a testimony to You today. Amen

---

Cease striving and know that I am God
— Psa. 46:10

If we are ever to experience growth in the Christian life we must stop holding ourselves back. Many of us impede our own growth by making one of two errors. There are a lot of us who like to hear the basics of the faith told over and over. That gives us plenty of shouting time but little else. There are a lot of us who read and listen to those who would make the faith a series of complicated exercises that leave us feeling inadequate as children of God. Trusting God and relishing His presence as we live our days in service to Him is incomprehensibly simple. Otherwise heaven would be only for the elite.

FATHER, I do trust You, but help me to trust You more. Amen

He chooses our inheritance for us — Psa. 47:4

Like children in a toy store we have difficulty deciding what we really want out of life. We want so many things and yet we are hesitant to release our grasp on anything we have for fear that some future thing might not be better. We want it all. But God wants for us that which is best. In His infinite wisdom and love He has prepared an inheritance for us that will cause our highest aspirations to appear as husks for swine. His grace has made us partakers of a glory which has been reserved only for Him throughout eternity. Through His Son we are heirs to heavens joys.

FATHER, help me to live today in the assurance of the inheritance You have prepared for me and which I have already begun to receive. Amen

---

We have thought on Thy lovingkindness, O God
— Psa. 48:9

When we think of God it is all too often in terms of what He can do for us. When we pray it is most often because of something we want. Is there not room in our thoughts to recall what God has already done? Is there no time in our prayers to give thanks for what God has already accomplished through His grace? Pondering the extent of God's mercy does a lot to help us put our lives into perspective. Considering the great love He has shown for us will put us into the proper relationship with God..

FATHER, when I consider Your works on my behalf I am driven to prostrate myself before Your mercy and I am lifted by Your love for me. Amen

———————

Why should I fear in days of adversity — Psa. 49:5

When trouble suddenly overwhelms us we seem to lose sight of everything but the problem that engulfs our life. The more we focus on the problem the more difficult it is to recognize a way out. We are paralyzed with fear and dread because our situation appears so hopeless. These are the times when we must be reminded, often by an outside source, that we have a remedy. As a child of God, we are never without hope. Because we live under the watchful eye of the One who loves us we are not overcome by circumstances. We know that the circumstances and forces that would harm us are under the constraint of our Father.

FATHER, when my eyes become focused on my problems today, lift my head so that I may see Your eyes of love. Amen

_____

He who offers a sacrifice of thanksgiving honors Me
— Psa. 50:23

So much of our doing for God falls into one of two categories. Either we do what we do because He told us to and we feel obligated, or we do our "good works" to please Him momentarily to get something we want from Him. Neither of these motives brings honor to our heavenly Father. We surely have reason to be thankful for what He has already done for us. Can we not serve Him simply out of a heart of gratitude for His mercy and grace? Would such service not please our Father more?

FATHER, I present my life to You today as an offering of thanksgiving. Amen

_____

Wash me thoroughly from my iniquity — Psa. 51:2

Why do we cling to sin so desperately? When we commit sinful acts we, of course, want to be forgiven. But we still want to claim the option to visit that sin again at some future time. We seem to want to keep some of the smudges of sin as proof that we are still "only human." However, when God forgives us and cleanses us, we are new again. Even those pesky lingering desires for that sin are removed from us. When real repentance has taken place we are going in a whole new direction with different options. God, in His mercy, removes even the desire for those things.

FATHER, cleanse me of those secret sins that You know all too well. Amen

---

Behold, the man who would not make God his refuge — Psa. 52:7

All to often we spend a lot of our time looking over our shoulder to see if the lost may be having more fun than we. Sometimes we may catch ourselves envying their wealth or power or glamorous lifestyle. But we need to take a closer look beneath the facade. The Bible teaches us that they are like graves that have been brightly decorated but are still filled with death. The future of the one who rejects faith in God is death, everlasting, separated from God. Look closely at the end when tempted to envy them now.

FATHER, remind me that I already have the best of life because I am being kept in Your care. Amen

---

God has looked . . . to see if there is anyone who understands — Psa. 53:2

Even a casual reading of Scripture enables you to see the numberless attempts by God to tell the world of the good news of His love for mankind. You can likewise see the countless times God warned His creation of the consequences of their continued rebellion against His love. From our perspective we might even wonder how they could have failed to see His mercy at work in the world. But we must also be humbled by the fact that Bible students in future generations will look back at us with the same kind of astonishment.

FATHER, help me not only to understand but to be willing to do something about my understanding. Amen

---

The Lord is the sustainer of my soul — Psa. 54:4

We live in an age of support groups. Whatever your situation in life there is a group that can encourage you, enlighten you, or just give you the satisfaction of belonging to a group. Some of these serve a good purpose. Most of all they allow people to understand that they are not alone. But these groups are not always around when your need is strongest. In many cases they can provide little more than commiseration. However, the Father is especially near in the time of our deepest need. His presence is our strength and hope.

FATHER, uphold me in the times of my weakness today so that I may be an encouragement to others. Amen

---

Cast your burden upon the Lord — Psa. 55:22

All of our lives we are taught to be self-sufficient. We look upon those who don't carry their own weight as slackers or bums. We give high marks to those who are "self-made." No wonder it is difficult for us to seek help in time of need. But some of our needs are beyond our strength yet our self-image demands that we do it ourselves. God has not promised to take away our hardships either. Instead, He has promised to give us wisdom and to bear us up when the trial is greater than human strength alone can bear.

FATHER, help me to seek Your wisdom to deal with my own burdens and the faith to trust You for those beyond my strength. Amen

---

*In God I have put my trust ... what can man
do to me? — Psa. 56:11*

Even the greatest saints of God have had those times when the threats of those around them have caused their faith to falter. Their circumstances caused them to lose their focus. Then the more they thought about the problem the bigger it seemed to become. But we remember those giants of the faith because in the final analysis their trust in God rose above all other considerations. After all it is God with whom we have our final meeting. For the believer it is there that his or her hope rests.

FATHER, may my faith in You triumph over any obstacle placed in my pathway today. Amen

---

In the shadow of Thy wings I will take refuge
— Psa. 57:1

All of us in these days are under attack. We are being pressed in on all sides. The pressures of living in an ungodly society, the pressures of a job that offers less and less security, the worries of providing well for family. We often seek a hiding place where we may get away from it all. What God offers us is not a place of escape but a foundation where we can take our stand and tap into His strength to face our foes. God is with us as we advance in the doing of His work in our world.

FATHER, I seek Your presence in my world today more than a place to hide from it. Amen

---

Surely there is a God who judges on the earth!
— Psa. 58:11

All too often in our day when we see great wrongs done or perhaps even suggested we cry out for justice but we also clamor for what we think that justice should be. Victims want the guilty punished to the maximum because that is what justice is to them. We are even guilty at times of rejoicing over the misfortune that comes to those we do not like and we consider that to be that just deserts. We seldom think of the bad things that come to us as the appropriate thing according to someone else. It would be good for us to remember that it is God who judges all of us.

FATHER, help me not to delight in judgment on others remembering that I too must appear before You daily. Amen

---

For Thou hast been my stronghold — Psa. 59:16

Most of us are aware that living the Christian life in today's world is like being an outpost surrounded by hostile forces. However, we must not allow ourselves to adopt a defensive posture even in these circumstances. Though we are under attack by Satan we are not under siege. Our supply line is Almighty God whose resources are without limit. Our defender and empowerer is the Holy Spirit of God. With our heavenly Father watching over us in love what need is there for fear?

FATHER, I thank You for the assurance of Your watch-care in all my circumstances today. Amen

---

Give us help ... for deliverance by man is in vain
— Psa. 60:11

When will we ever learn this? Of course we depend upon our friends for support in any time of trouble and that is as it should be. But there are limits to what they can do. Some of our circumstances are beyond their ability to be of real help. However, no matter what our friends may or may not do, our ultimate deliverer is our almighty Father. He alone is the one who can save us from ourselves and our sin. Mankind may provide limited assistance, but God can and does being salvation.

FATHER, I call on You for my deliverance again today. Amen

Thou hast given me the inheritance of those who fear Thy name — Psa. 61:5

So many believers are fearful of their salvation. They are paralyzed in their witness and in their life by the nagging concern that they have missed something in the formula for being saved. Surely God never intended our relationship with Him to be so uncertain. Surely He wants for us, not the assumption of the arrogant, but the confidence of a child. The psalmist speaks of this assurance by affirming his own place among those who trust God and who consequently are heirs of God.

FATHER, I thank You today that I am Yours and You are mine. Amen

---

My soul, wait in silence for God only — Psa. 62:5

How can we wait? Voices and noises all around us clamor for our attention or simply drown out what needs our attention. Our culture requires a lot of waiting but cannot abide waiting. We must be moving. We need answers now. We want everything now. When we pray, we want God to do for us NOW. But the prophet Elijah learned centuries ago that God is not always found amid the hubbub. To hear Him and know His presence we must turn aside and be aware of His voice in the gentle stillness. Being with Him in such a way brings peace to our spirit and renewed strength to our soul.

FATHER, remind me to step aside from the whir of my busy-ness so that my soul can know that blessed quietness of fellowship with You today. Amen

---

My soul thirsts for Thee, my flesh yearns for Thee
— Psa. 63:1

Few of us have ever known real thirst or hunger. We have had a dry mouth or heard our stomach growl, but have not had near delirium that comes with prolonged lack of those nutrients essential to the body. By the same token few of us have known a hunger and thirst for the righteousness of God. We have not felt such a spiritual need. Could it be that much of the doldrums we know in the spirit are caused by our feeling already satisfied and no longer yearning after God?

FATHER, renew my longing for You in all my activities today. Amen

---

Their own tongue is against them — Psa. 64:8

The Bible aptly reminds us that our tongue, though small, exerts tremendous power over our lives. With it we have the ability to build up or tear down. We can inspire others with our words or demoralize them. We can provide guidance or mislead. We can speak the truth or a counterfeit of the truth. However, when we choose to use our tongues against others we discover that we injure ourselves in the process. Surely God will hold us accountable for words we so thoughtlessly or hurtfully utter. It is as though the tongue's sharpest points are on the user end.

FATHER, help to use my words only to bless today. Amen

By awesome deeds Thou dost answer us in righteousness — Psa. 65:5

We easily get into the habit of not expecting much from God. Oh, we know He has great power and that He can do marvelous things. But so long as our life is moving along on a fairly even keel we don't give much thought to our need for the mighty power of God. Yet it is precisely because of His continuing powerful activity on our behalf that life remains mostly smooth for us. He intervenes for us in countless ways that may never catch our attention unless our eyes are open to His work. His powerful and loving arms bear us along each moment of the day.

FATHER, open my eyes today to Your mighty works on my behalf. Amen

---

I will tell of what He has done for my soul — Psa. 66:16

We need not strain our minds to think of something good that God has done for us. We don't tax our memories to recall some undeserved blessing our heavenly Father has brought to us. Not the least of His blessings has been the gift of His Son to pay the penalty for our sin and restore us to fellowship with Him. Add to that the proffer of His strength and wisdom for the living of each day. To that we must also add His promise of life everlasting in His presence. How could we not tell others of the wonderful things God has done for us?

FATHER, may my life today give testimony to Your goodness to me. Amen

---

Let the nations be glad ... for Thou wilt judge
— Psa. 67:4

We are not always comforted to think of God in terms of judge. It may be caused by our general fear of appearing before any judge. Each of us certainly is aware of the wrongdoing in our life. Even the best of us can manage some feelings of guilt when we are called to account. We also have that nagging fear that judges sometimes make mistakes. But with God there will be no mistake in our case. He can always be counted on for justice. More important than that is the fact that the Judge before whom we live our whole life is One for whom justice is founded upon His mercy towards creatures He gave His Son's life for.

FATHER, I do not cringe before Your judgment because I am kept in Your love. Amen

---

Only the rebellious dwell in a parched land
— Psa. 68:6

All of us experience those times in life when circumstances have brought discouragement and heartbreak. Those times have taken away a measure of our happiness for a time. But our continued faithfulness maintains a deep-seated joy that is able to lift us and keep our life fruitful for God and others. On the other hand are those broken by circumstances who turn their backs on God and on life. For them there is no restoration. No inner peace can they find that is able to soften their dry soul and bring life again to their spirits.

FATHER, as I open my heart to You today I am confident that You will send Your spiritual rain to restore my soul once again. Amen

---

O God, it is Thou who dost know my folly
— Psa. 69:5

Though we may successfully hide it for a while our sin always does find us out. When those who trust us learn of it they are disappointed and we are embarrassed. When those against us learn of it they are reaffirmed and we are embarrassed. But neither our friends nor our enemies ever know the real depth of our wrongdoing. They seldom notice more than the symptoms. Only God is aware of how much our "folly" has permeated our soul. Only our heavenly

Father knows the extent to which our very spirit has become infected. But it is our Father who stands ready to make us whole.

FATHER, because You know my heart I trust my sin to You today. Amen

———————

Let all who seek Thee rejoice and be glad
— Psa. 70:4

All too often we have made the search for God a tedious and complicated procedure requiring some special knowledge or technique. In doing so we often cause a lot of seekers to become frustrated and even give up hope. But what many of us have discovered is that when we decide to turn from our life of sin we find ourselves at His feet. The long and treacherous part of our journey is the time we have spent going our own way which is the way of sin and death. When we turn toward God we have reason to "rejoice and be glad" because our search is over.

FATHER, my heart fills with joy when I recall that You have been pursuing me in love since I first turned into the path of sin. Amen

———————

Thou hast given commandment to save me
— Psa. 71:3

Having influence with someone who is in power can often be of great benefit. Knowing someone who knows someone can cut through a lot of red tape in our society. But because of the One who loves us and the Intercessor seated at His right hand we have more than influence. Our heavenly Father who rules over all has issued a decree that all who are His will work in cooperation to preserve all who are His. In seeking to do God's will we must continually work together for the mutual good of all God's children.

FATHER, I thank You today for Your work through others on my behalf and for the privilege of serving You by also serving them. Amen

---

He will deliver ... him who has no helper — 72:12

Like a growing child we have those times in our lives when we think we can take care of ourselves without help from anyone. We like the feeling of independence. But when we come to understand that such freedom leaves us alone and isolated we also begin to see that some situations in life are beyond us. When we realize that we are helpless we may become panic-stricken unless we understand that It is just such people that God has always been trying to deliver from themselves. No one is without a deliverer because God lives and cares for His creation.

FATHER, even in my lonely times today remind me of Your constant care for me. Amen

---

Besides Thee, I desire nothing on earth
— Psa. 73:25

Someone crawling across the desert sands whose throat is parched and tongue swollen from thirst surely has only one thought in mind and that is water. A person dying of hunger would do almost anything for a scrap of bread. Has your soul ever been so thirsty for God that all other considerations fade into insignificance? Jesus once said that any person who desires God like this will be filled. Yet we continue to nibble the edges of the blessings of God and wonder why we never know the overflowing joy of life in Him.

FATHER, lead me to desire more of You in everything I do today. Amen

---

Thy congregation, which Thou hast purchased
of old — Psa. 74:2

Young love is a sweet thing to watch; but old love that has endured the hardships of life is a magnificent tribute to love itself. Our love relationship with God is not a new thing, at least with God. His love has proven itself from the beginning of time when He came in love for the first sinners. That intended intimacy with all of humanity has broken forth at every turn of history. His love for a special people has continued down through the centuries. His special love was demonstrated when He paid the awful price on Calvary. Now we who have been purchased stand before Him as sons and daughters.

FATHER, remind me today that You purchased me to be an heir and not a slave. Amen

---

God is the Judge — Psa. 75:7

We use so much of our emotional energy in concern over what other people, even strangers, think of how we look, how we dress, or the way we do our job. We work hard to make a good impression. We want our church friends to think we're a good Christian. A good appearance from any perspective is what we hope for. But our efforts are mostly wasted on the wrong people. Our real concern should be to make a good impression on our heavenly Father. That impression is made by a heart inclined to righteousness.

FATHER, help me to be more concerned about Your view of me than what others think. Amen

---

The wrath of man shall praise Thee — Psa. 76:10

Bringing praise to God is the highest function of humankind. All of creation itself gives praise to the power and majesty of God. The intricate detail of even the smallest creature praises the care of God for all of creation. The work of God in Christ Jesus has given praise to the love of God in giving new life to those who trust Him. And the continued existence of those who reject God and fight against Him gives praise to the mercy and patience of God. Indeed all creation offers up praise for the goodness of God for He alone is worthy.

FATHER, may my life today give praise for Your mercy to me in Jesus. Amen

---

In the day of my trouble I sought the Lord
— Psa. 77:2

It seems the way of all flesh that we should always be God's "foul weather friends." Rather than seek Him out when life is good and we are enjoying His blessings to the full, we turn toward Him when our life has fallen apart. God desires fellowship with us in the good times but He welcomes us at those other times as well. Our heavenly Father loves us and longs for us to be near Him. Sometimes I have wondered if maybe He allows us to get into a mess so that we will come running to Him. But is it not tragic that we must get ourselves into trouble before we remember who loves us and wants to come to our aid?

FATHER, I come to You with joy today not waiting for trouble to drive me toward Your care. Amen

---

Tell to the generation to come the praises of the Lord — Psa. 78:4

The Scriptures graphically portray for us the danger of allowing our witness dying with us. We cannot make the next generation believe in the God of our fathers and of us. They alone are responsible for that. Our function is to tell. And the best way we can pass along our faith is by telling what God has done for us. When our passion for Christ bursts forth in praise our words are given more credence. When our life for Christ bears the imprint of His character then our words about Him can be believed.

FATHER, may my life today be aglow with Your light and break forth in praise of Your love for me. Amen

---

Let Thy compassion come quickly to meet us — Psa. 79:8

As our modern world moves forward each day it has a habit of leaving many casualties in its wake. Those who hesitate to adapt to the constant changes are pushed aside. The ones considered liabilities are isolated. At one time or another each of us could be that liability. Each day we feel some of the crush of the hectic pace of the world around us. In such hurried times we want a hurried response from God. We need His merciful presence and we need it now.

We need to remind ourselves that the compassionate presence of God is always with us.

FATHER, I thank You for Your constant care even in those times when I am unaware of my need. Amen

---

Cause Thy face to shine upon us, and we will be saved — Psa. 80:19

The favor of friends and loved ones is indeed a blessing to any person. Knowing that we have their support in our endeavors gives us added energy for our task. Having the esteem of those outside our circle of friends can certainly provide a boost to one's confidence and encouragement to the work one must do. But to know the smile of God is greater still. History has shown that the blessing of His favor does more than encourage. It, in fact, empowers us for the work we do. Whatever the gloom of our circumstances, or drudgery of our labor. They are brightened and made meaningful by the loving presence of our God.

FATHER, in spite of my current circumstances I will glory in Your favor today. Amen

---

Oh that My people would listen to Me — Psa. 81:13

Far too many times we worry about God not answering our prayers or not speaking to us. We call ourselves seeking His face and wanting to hear a word from

Him. The problem has never been an unwillingness on the part of God to speak to our heart. The Father has not been dilenquent to answer our pleas. The Holy One has not been sulking in silence even because of our sin. His end of the line has always been open. The problem has always been us. We have refused to hear Him or our sin has clogged the lines of communication. Our loving Father longs to speak from His heart fo ours if we would only listen.

FATHER, help me to be attentive to Your voice today. Amen

Rescue the weak and needy — Psa. 82:4

For many years now there has been a movement in religious circles that appears to lay aside all spiritual concerns and consider meeting physical needs as the fulfillment of all their religious duties. Many if not most Christians rejected that notion. However, many of us now find it is so easy for us to wrap ourselves in "spiritual" activity and absolve ourselves of more mundane things like caring for those around us who are in physical need. We often forget that God did not so much call us to gather together as He did send us out into the world caring as He has cared in Jesus.

FATHER, deliver me from such a focus on my heavenly future that I am unable to see the real needs around me here and now. Amen

---

O God, do not remain quiet — Psa. 83:1

It never fails. We feel no isolation from God when the circumstances of life are going our way. There is no longing in our heart to hear His voice so long as we are facing no problems. But it does seem that when trials come we quickly experience a void. We often begin to notice a silence or a distance from God. So many thoughts and noises from our troubled situation compete for our attention, the calm, assuring voice of God is drowned out. In those times it may take more effort to hear the encouraging word from the Father. In those times we need to quiet ourselves so that His word can come to us.

FATHER, still those noises around me that obscure and garble Your words to me today. Amen

---

No good thing does He withhold from those who walk uprightly — Psa. 84:11

The way we often pray it is as though the God to whom we pray must be persuaded with great fervor to part with even the smallest of His blessings. Such a miserly heavenly Father must be approached with something like a secret formula by one who has taken all the right steps and promised all the right things. Surely this is not the Father who loved us so much that He would give His own Son for creatures who had turned their backs on Him. The Father who gave

Jesus to His rebellious children would not hold back lesser things.

FATHER, I thank You that Your hand is always open to me because I have trusted You. Amen

---

I will hear what God the Lord will say — *Psa. 85:8*

Most people I know are just so busy. We have our jobs, our hobbies, our families, our churches with each demanding more time even when there is no more. In the midst of all these demands we rightly feel that we cannot squeeze anything else into our life. My parents always told me that you always have time for those matters that are most important to you. If we believe that God's point of view is important to our life then we will make time for hearing what He has to say. This includes not only listening but also doing what He says.

FATHER, I open my life to listening and doing Your good pleasure this day. Amen

---

Thou, Lord, art good, and ready to forgive
— Psa. 86:5

This is such an amazing contrast in our heavenly Father, that He can both be good and forgiving at the same time. Much of the time what passes for good among us has great difficulty in looking on the "not good" with any degree of compassion. We rail against them and their actions rather than trying to look upon them in love and mercy. We good ones declare that we "hate the sin and love the sinner" when in fact the focus of our dislike is not that good. It seems that only God has that good an aim. I certainly am glad because sometimes even our "good" is tainted with the sin that so easily besets us.

FATHER, open my compassion to others as You have done for me. Amen

---

The Most High Himself will establish — Psa. 87:5

We can often whip ourselves into a frenzy of activity in an effort to complete a project that is important to us. Some tasks we willingly undertake without consideration of pay. We believe so strongly in the endeavor that we are determined that it succeed. But no matter how many hours of our time, no matter how many dollars, we give to a project, its success is still not guaranteed. Even when these commitments are made to a church project success is still not certain. The Scriptures teach us that the power behind any such project must be God or even the "success" of it will be a failure.

FATHER, I commit myself to include you at the beginning and in every step of anything I wish to do in Your service today. Amen

---

My soul has had enough trouble — Psa. 88:3

As we read such a passage we quickly want to say a hearty "AMEN!" No matter how good our lives may have been many of us tend to look more at the negatives of life than the brighter side. For sure it is the down side of life that most often drives us to God's throne in prayer. But we usually don't bother God with all the irritants of life. We wait until they build to the point of frustration and then we dump them all at His feet in disgust. On the other hand, the real struggles of life lead us into His presence with the joy of knowing that in that place we always find strength and relief. The saints of all the ages who have known the ravages of spiritual warfare have also borne the marks of that unshakable joy.

FATHER, teach me that Your love for me transcends any trouble I may face today. Amen

---

How blessed are the people who know the joyful sound! — Psa. 89:15

In times of trouble and conflict it is difficult to break forth in songs of joy. In the midst of trying circumstances such expressions would be rank hypocrisy. But regardless of our present situation we have received the glorious promises of the Gospel. The assurances we have from the heavenly Father bring us joy in the midst of the storms of life. Other religious expressions lead to contemplation or even fear, but our faith puts a song in our heart. Through the work of Jesus Christ in the world and in our lives we have been given that "joy unspeakable and full of glory" and we must sing. Mere words could not do it justice.

FATHER, help me to make the song in my heart the guiding force in all that I do today. Amen

---

Confirm for us the work of our hands — Psa. 90:17

When we work hard at anything we want to see results. This is a part of our culture. We are unwilling to leave the results or the appreciation of our efforts to some future generation. But service for God does not always, or even often, have immediate, tangible results. We want and need affirmation to strengthen us for further service. How will others know that we have been faithful without these measurable results? Sometimes we may feel that the lack of visible results is a lack of God's approval. But the Scriptures give us countless examples of men and women who labored long for the Master receiving only His secret smile to give them strength for their task.

FATHER, thank You for the affirmation of Your loving presence with me today. Amen

---

I will rescue him, and honor him — Psa. 91:15

This psalm is for those days when everything else seems to go wrong, when no one seems to be your friend, when your whole world appears to be alien to you. During those times we are tempted to wonder if God has turned a deaf ear to our cries for help. We want deliverance and exaltation now so that those around us may see that we are one of God's choice servants. But even if our heavenly Father were to be our only fan, would that not be sufficient? If our rescue and honor must wait for heaven's great gathering will that not be enough? The promise of God is that deliverance and honor will come from Him and that is really all we need.

FATHER, I submit my circumstances today to You so that I may learn again that You are the only blessing I really need. Amen

---

It is good to give thanks to the Lord — Psa. 92:1

As a species, humans are an ungrateful lot. We are the very crown of creation, the ones made in the image of God, the target of redemption even at the cost of God's Son. But most remain unthankful. But it is important that we give thanks for any and all blessings. When we do not demonstrate thankfulness we take God's blessings as a given. We become callous toward His benefits as though they are a normal part of life. Being thankful, on the other hand, opens our eyes to more of the blessings He is giving us. When we give thanks we open the windows of heaven for Him to bless us even more.

FATHER, I thank You for the blessing of an expectant heart. Amen

---

Thy testimonies are fully confirmed — Psa. 93:5

Over the centuries many have looked at certain horrible events and concluded that there must not be a God or such things would never happen. This is especially true of some who were going through those troubles at the time. However, some have come to that conclusion from a detachment brought on by generations of relatively trouble-free existence. However, for most people who have walked this globe, there is a daily confrontation with wonders that insist that there not only is a God but that He is obviously One who cares for this world. Start your day with praise by taking a moment to observe the handiwork of the God of heaven and earth all around You.

FATHER, early in the morning my song shall rise to Thee. Amen

---

Thy consolations delight my soul — Psa. 94:19

The Scriptures teach and demonstrate that God is continually working for the good of His children in the midst of all the circumstances of life. On those occasions when we take our eyes off the troubles that beset us we are able to see those efforts of God on our behalf. When we are able to see Him bringing His blessings to us in those times our soul is certainly made glad. Is it any wonder that we feel bubbling up inside us that well of joy that is unspeakable and full of His glory.

FATHER, I thank You today for the many little bits of Your glory that keep popping into my life when I begin to feel down. Amen

---

Let us come before His presence with thanksgiving
— Psa. 95:2

Throughout the history of humanity it has been important to most that they be able to present themselves before God. Most deities kept their followers in fear and had to be appeased before it was safe to come before them. Even those who worship the one true God have often come to Him in fear. But our God, the Father of the Lord Jesus Christ has invited us to come boldly unto His throne. That invitation and the knowledge that we have of the love of God shown us in Christ Jesus does make it possible for us to approach Him with thanksgiving in our heart.

FATHER, because of Your love for me my heart overflow with thanksgiving at the very thought of You. Amen

---

Tell of His glory among the nations — Psa. 96:3

What a responsibility we have! To think that there are so many all around us who do not know the truth of Jesus that can deliver them from eternal damnation is overwhelming. To recall that we are the only instruments God has to get the message to them is almost frightening. But what a privilege we have! To think that God has made us participants in His glorious act of redemption is humbling. To think that our Deliverer has chosen us to have the opportunity of bringing the Good News to a world in such desperate need is a great challenge. His command to tell is really only giving us permission to do what we can't help doing.

FATHER, thank you for encouraging me to do what I really don't want to leave undone. Amen

---

All the peoples have seen His glory — Psa. 97:6

The glory of God is all around us. Created in the image of God, His glory is even in us. But, not looking for God, people often see that glory and ascribe it to someone or something else. The Father has been exposing Himself to humanity since the dawn of time and yet He has largely been ignored. No wonder the Apostle could say that such people are "without excuse." Compounding that tragedy is the fact that we as believers have not careful to properly attribute glory to God. We must take care to allow the glory to shine as His and not anyone else's.

FATHER, may I point others to Your glory in all things today. Amen

---

He is coming to judge the earth — Psa. 98:9

What a frightening prospect to think of the holy and righteous Creator of the universe coming to call His creatures to an accounting! It causes us to ponder our behavior and recall the sins that so easily besets us. We are made to remember the countless times we have failed our Lord. When we think about all those occasions in which we have dishonored His name we have reason to be fearful of His coming. BUT, when we remember the wonderful change He has made in our life because of the redemptive work of Jesus, we can welcome His coming as of a Father coming to gather His children.

FATHER, thank You for being Father and Savior to me. Amen

Thou wast a forgiving God to them — Psa. 99:8

We have all wasted valuable time and energy being crippled by some sin we have committed and felt ashamed of. Sometimes we are afraid our friends might find out. But more than that we are fearful and ashamed that God knows and that we have cut ourselves off from Him. God is angered when we do things that hurt us, hurt others, and damage our relationship with Him. One of sins most hurtful effects is the shame or the hardness that keeps us from setting it right with Him immediately. God is always eager to forgive us and cleanse us.

FATHER, remind me today to run to You when I have fallen and hurt myself and others. Amen

---

Serve the Lord with gladness — Psa. 100:2

The sour looks seen on the faces in your church on Sunday mornings are a disgrace to the Gospel. Disgruntled attitudes from Christians in the workplace on Monday mornings are surely a shame to the Lord we represent. Christians are not expected to smile all the time, even our Lord was not like that. But undergirding every moment of the day for a believer is that unshakable joy which is the bedrock of our faith. Perhaps the most believable aspect of our Christian testimony is that gladness with which we go about our work because whatever our chore we may offer it up as a service to God.

FATHER, I commit myself to Your service through each thing I am called upon to do today. Amen

---

I will set no worthless thing before my eyes
— Psa. 101:3

Gross immorality is not a problem for most believers. It is, rather, those small "indiscretions" that trouble us. Perhaps even worse than those is the time we give to thoughts and activities that are of no value to ourselves or others. Many of you were told early in your life that "an idle mind is the devil's workshop." It is certainly true that when our minds are disengaged from fruitful endeavors they too easily slip into thoughts and behavior that are not a credit to our faith. Like a car on a hill needs active effort to keep from going downhill, our minds must be involved in wholesome thought or it will surely sink into unworthy ones.

FATHER, help me to keep my mind from idle clutter by focusing my thoughts on You. Amen

―――――――――――

He has regarded the prayer of the destitute
— Psa. 102:17

One of the great tragedies of most religious people is that they do not seek their god until they have nowhere else to turn. Even in the Christian faith, prayer is seldom used until all other options have been expended. Our God who has all the power and authority and always uses it for our good is usually ignored until we have a problem. Does that make any sense to you? We can be thankful that our heavenly

Father is long-suffering. We can be grateful that He loves us so much that He is willing to wait on us. When we have gotten so deep into our mess that we can see no other way out and then turn to the One who is the Way, He is ready and able to hear and answer.

FATHER, I long for Your nearness today regardless of my circumstances. Amen

---

He has not dealt with us according to our sins
— Psa. 103:10

Often we are able to be almost casual about our sin. We have not done terrible things like murder. We are basically pretty good people. But once in a while we need to remind ourselves of the cost of our sins to us, to others, and especially to God. The Bible tells us that the "wages of sin is death." But God, through the work of His Son Jesus through the cross and the resurrection, has made it possible for us to live. Though we had all earned death God has given us everlasting life. As a part of that life He has made us acceptable in His sight and has promised us His fellowship throughout eternity. What a merciful God is our heavenly Father!

FATHER, I worship You today because of all Your tender mercies toward me. Amen

---

Let my meditation be pleasing to Him
— Psa. 104:34

We believers are so proud of ourselves when we have kept our public behavior circumspect. We can become positively smug about living a life of high moral character both publicly and in the privacy of our home. We sometimes even allow ourselves to point a finger at those whose public or private lives shame them. But we seem to forget that God does not judge us solely according to our actions. Before the bar of God we are judged on the basis of the thoughts and intents of our heart. We are often guilty of trying to keep the outward clean as a disguise for thoughts and desires that are inconsistent with what we profess.

FATHER, guard my thoughts today that they may be worthy of one who is Your child. Amen

---

Make known His deeds among the peoples
— Psa. 105:1

"I can't wait to tell you!" We become so excited about some events in our lives we are fairly bursting to spread the news. We want others to be just as excited as we are. Something has happened in our life and we simply must tell it to everyone we know. How incredible it is that it is seemingly so easy for us to hold in the best thing that ever happened to us, our deliverance from the ravages of sin in this life and the one to come. How tragic that this life-changing information should be kept from those whose future is so desolate!

FATHER, help me to make known the source of my joy to those around me today. Amen

———————————

We have sinned like our fathers — Psa. 106:6

Each generation of humanity hopes to progress in its civilization, building on the gains of those who went before. Yet some of the gains are always in the wrong direction. Our capacity for sin does not seem to lessen with the passage of time. We may look upon former times as being brutish and they were; but we as a human race have only become more sophisticated in our sin and not one wit more righteous than our forebears. Being good is not just a matter of trying to be better than we are. Instead it is a matter of following the guidance of our heavenly Father.

FATHER, help me to be more obedient so that I can be good. Amen

———————————

The hungry soul He has filled with what is good
— Psa. 107:9

Most of us, like children who are picky eaters, simply have little appetite for the good things with which God wants to feed us. Only a few things do we allow ourselves from God's great banquet table. Others of us gorge ourselves on the world's snacks that satisfy us only temporarily leaving us craving for more with the same outcome. All the while God has prepared a feast for us of the things our souls need and we have so jaded our spiritual taste buds that we have no desire for His food. But those who yearn for the food of God will be satisfied by Him.

FATHER, help me to realize that You alone are the bread and drink that will satisfy. Amen

––––––––––––––

Through God we shall do valiantly — Psa. 108:13

"I can't do it." We have all said that at some time or other. When faced with a challenge that stretches our resources to the limit we may throw up our hands in frustration or flop down in despair. Our energy and determination simply are not enough for the task. But then in the closet of our minds where we stash everything we think we might need at some future time we discover God. We often keep Him there during the good times because we can do things on our own. Then we are reminded that only when we work in the strength of Almighty God are we assured victory.

FATHER, my desire is to start each project of this day by seeking Your strength. Amen

––––––––––––––

Let them know that this is Thy hand — *Psa. 109:27*

Over the centuries mankind has wrongly attributed many things to God simply because they were unexplainable. Everything that happened was considered God's will. On the other hand, many of the good things in life were wrongly attributed to "luck" or our own wisdom. It is important for us to remember that every good thing has its origin in God. It is also important that we help others to understand that all the blessings we enjoy have come from the hand of our loving Father.

FATHER, remind me that everything I have that is worth having is most valuable because it had its origin in Your love for me. Amen

---

The people will volunteer freely — *Psa. 110:3*

One of the tragic facts of modern-day church life is the shortage of people for doing the work of the church. Many church workers are drafted and some are dragged into service by being made to feel guilty. Is serving God and His church that distasteful? Is it really such a burden to do the work of the Lord? Nothing is too burdensome for those we love. Since we profess love to Christ, how is it that we find it so tiresome to give ourselves to His service? Perhaps our love has grown cold or we really don't love Him at all.

FATHER, help me to find my true joy in willingly serving You. Amen

---

The fear of the Lord is the beginning of wisdom
— Psa. 110:10

The act of learning is a beautiful thing to watch. Parents observing their young children at play or teachers seeing their students finally grasping a concept feel a burst of joy at another stage of development. There is so much to be learned. We are bombarded with and overwhelmed by the flood of information that comes our way each day. Yet as we look around us amid this tide of information we find a dramatic decrease in wisdom. Wisdom is the ability to rightly use the information at hand. That ability comes only from God who is able to help us understand. He gives that to all who own Him as Lord.

FATHER, I lay myself at Your feet again today as an offering of service to You. Amen

---

Light arises in the darkness for the upright
— Psa. 112:4

Most of the inhabitants of the earth live all their lives in the darkness of sin and trouble. We know that such is their lot apart from Christ. But many Christians seem not to be able to handle the fact that times of trial and darkness come even for believers.

When those times do come many are shattered and their faith nearly crumbles. But the Scriptures teach us that it is in those very times that God is at work bringing about good to those of us who love Him. For the believer there is the special promise that God turns the shadows of night into the morning.

FATHER, remind me that even my dark times have been made light by Your presence. Amen

---

He raised the poor from the dust — Psa. 113:7

One of the most heartening aspects of the Gospel for me is the fact that those who may be cast aside or disenfranchised by society are still not outside the care of God. None of us can be so unworthy that God's love is unavailable to us. This is surely grace. But the demand side of the Gospel would teach us that our own love and care as believers must certainly be directed to those same unwanted ones. Our compassion and determination toward them has, since the days of the prophets, been a sign of our commitment to God.

FATHER, remind me to reach out my hand in Your name to those who are in need. Amen

---

Judah became His sanctuary — Psa. 114:2

Why was one chosen for honor instead of another? This is the kind of question always lurking in the minds of those seeking prominence in any field of endeavor. When the selection has been made we sometimes are critical of the one who bestows the honor and even of the one who receives it. But those honored by God must keep in mind that in His grace there is no merit and in His love there is no need. What comes to us from the hand of God is always and only His mercy and grace. Our chosenness is a delight to our heart but the honor must always go to God.

FATHER, I am delighted and humbled today that You have chosen to dwell in me. Amen

---

Not to us, O Lord ... but to Thy name give glory
— Psa. 115:1

Most of us who are considered mentally healthy are more likely to accept credit than blame. When the pleasant outcome is really no more than fluke we are willing to credit our skill, our planning, or our hard work. Even in doing the work of God we are too often likely to honor some human instrument rather than God. When we do give the credit to God it is often done in such a way that those who hear us rightly assume that it is only an attempt at modesty. But in our hearts we know that any good thing done had its origins in God and He can use the vilest of His creation as instruments for that good.

FATHER, all I will seek for my service today is the smile of Your good pleasure. Amen

---

Thou hast rescued my soul from death — Psa. 116:8

Each of us has met countless people in our lifetime. Some of them became our friends for a time. But if we go for a long time without contact with them we forget their face and often even their name. However, one who was involved in the crucial times of our life is almost impossible to forget. The person who has saved your life could surely not be forgotten. Our heavenly Father who has redeemed us from hell must surely be in our thoughts at all times. How then do we seem to lose Him amid the clutter of our busy day?

FATHER, keep before me today the truth that You have given me my life and everything good in it. Amen

---

The truth of the Lord is everlasting — Psa. 117:2

We are accustomed to temporariness in everything. Lifetime guarantees are understood by most as an advertising gimmick and "till death do us part" promises are no more than relic ritual with no real meaning in these modern days. "Truth" is understood as little more than today's fact that will be replaced by tomorrow's discovery. But our Lord declared that though everything else may fade into obscurity with time His truth does not diminish. What He says to us and about us has not changed and we still cannot escape it.

FATHER, open my eyes and ears to that truth which You are still speaking to me. Amen

---

The Lord answered me and set me in a large place
— Psa. 118:5

We have so filled our world with tight schedules, pressing workloads, and cramped living areas there is little wonder we feel hemmed in and stressed out. The strictures we have imposed on life are surely enough to make us implode, self-destruct, or explode, and destroy those around us. But the amazing fact of living in God's world and as His child is that even in the most confining circumstances we are liberated by our understanding of our continuing relationship to Christ. He has truly set us free from all the ties that would frustrate and defeat us.

FATHER, I relish, today, the air of freedom you allow me to breathe as I live in Your presence. Amen

---

Who seek Him with all their heart — Psa. 119:2

Half-heartedness is rampant in our world today. Commitment to country, to family, to ideals, or to God has been waning through most of our life. It appears that we are willing to commit to persons or to concepts only so long as those allegiances do not incur significant cost to us. The idea seems to be that we will reap all the advantages of being on the fringes of real relationship without the responsibilities inherent in a deeper commitment. For that reason many professing believers have never known the overflowing joy that wells up within the heart of one who stakes all on knowing Christ.

FATHER, help me to keep You as the priority in my life today. Amen

---

Open my eyes that I may behold — Psa. 119:18

Like many people, I am a morning person. To be able to start fresh with a new day given to me by God with its limitless possibilities is both a challenge and a great joy. No starting the day with a negative view of the inherent dangers for me. This is not a mater of optimism but a matter of the hope we have in Jesus Christ. But to come near the close of what might have been a grueling day of work and be able still to have your eyes open with wonder at the limitless possibilities for what God can do with your circumstances for that day is truly a joy unspeakable.

FATHER, continue to open my eyes and cleanse my vision so that I may glimpse Your mighty hand at work in my life. Amen

---

Revive me according to Thy word — Psa. 119:25

The Lord Jesus promised His followers a kind of life that surged up from within their souls like an artesian well that would not run dry and could not be capped off by circumstances. But all of us have gone through those periods of life when we felt dry and lifeless in the spirit and for a while could not determine why. Yet we knew the source of those living waters even when we seemed unable tot gain access. In those times of great spiritual thirst our souls cried out and God always heard our prayer. When we truly desire Him He provides that which gives our souls new life.

FATHER, deliver me from searching for something to revitalize my life because I know that each moment I need Your life in mine lest I die. Amen

---

Turn away my eyes from looking at vanity
— Psa. 119:37

It is so easy to get caught up in ourselves. Our culture encourages us to look to ourselves. But vanity is more than a matter of personal appearance. Vanity has to do with any of those pursuits in life that have little or no lasting value. How much of our normal day deals with "trivial pursuits?" We must all confess that much of our energy, time, and money is spent on activities that are of little importance. Perhaps it would be worthwhile for each of us to take a second look at what we are about and be sure that we focus on those things that are really significant for us and for those who look to us.

FATHER, deliver me over to activities that are worthy of me as a child of Yours. Amen

---

I will walk at liberty — Psa. 119:45

Very few of us have had the experience of being confined to a prison cell or even to a bed for an extended period. But worse than this confinement is something we all know about. Rebellion against God and His purpose for us (sin) have a way of building walls and forming shackles for us. In our freedom from God we imprison ourselves in a lifestyle that separates us from all that is good for us. In our slavery to self and sin we so tightly restrict ourselves that we imagine that this is the way life is. But when the One who holds the key to life, death, and eternity comes to rescue us we are free indeed.

FATHER, thank You for the liberty I received when I submitted myself to You. Amen

---

In which Thou hast made me hope — Psa. 119:49

The older we get the easier it becomes to have a more cynical view of life. You find that hard work is not always what gets you ahead on your job and even good friends can disappoint you. A healthy pessimism may appear to be the only reasonable attitude toward life in this world. But our heavenly Father has given us reason for something other than a negative outlook on life. Through our faith in Him we have more than the possibility for hope. His actions toward us have given us no choice but hope.

FATHER, I give thanks to You that what I see around me today will not take away my hope in You. Amen

---

I considered my ways, and turned my feet
— Psa. 119:59

Modern society has become accustomed to much introspection. We usually spend so much time looking at ourselves that we hardly take thought of others. This kind of self-examination quite often leads to a loss of self-esteem or an inflated self-image. Only when our look at ourselves is through the special lens provided by God can it really be beneficial. When God shows us what we truly are we can see the need for change. When God bestows His grace then we have the power for that change.

FATHER, open my eyes to what I am and open my heart to receive Your cleansing grace. Amen

---

It is good for me that I was afflicted — Psa. 119:71

Can we honestly say that? On the surface it sounds almost masochistic, as though we have gotten some sort of pleasure from our pain. But that is not the case or else we would be sick. Rather, this refers to the pains of life from which we learn. Trials and afflictions are the rule of earthly life. From them we receive the discipline and lessons of life through which we mature. We need not blame all our pains on God. But through those "irritants" God has promised that He will work good for those of us who love Him.

FATHER, show me Your hand at work in my circumstances today for my good. Amen

---

Thy hands made me and fashioned me
— Psa. 119:73

The tremendous discoveries made by modern science in this century simply boggle the mind of most of us. They have explained for us mortals many of the things once shrouded in mystery in the consequent fear of the unknown. As a result of this, though, many of these exposed processes have become somewhat mundane. However, as believers we still stand in awe even at these revelations of facts because we know

116

that behind them is the hand of God who set these processes in motion and continues to guide them in His love and mercy. We must remember that we are just as surely formed by the hand of God as were Adam and Eve at the beginning.

FATHER, I thank You for the assurance that You continue to make me and fashion me each day. Amen

---

My soul languishes for Thy salvation — Psa. 119:81

Few, if any, of us has ever been truly hungry or thirsty. Few have pined for anyone or anything to the point of being unable to function. A small number of us lived such a long time in sin and then sought desperately for God. Most of us were reared in Christian homes and came to the faith early in our lives. But there are also many of us who have gone through those long dry places in our spiritual lives where we seemed alienated from God and His power because of some sin or some perceived failure in His service. We ache to know again the warmth of His presence and the nourishment of His Spirit. And He was with us all the while.

FATHER, when my spiritual knees buckle with the weight of Your service, remind me that I am not in this work alone. Amen

---

Thy word is settled in heaven — Psa. 119:89

We all remember hearing about the days when "a man's word was his bond." I doubt that there ever was really such a time. We have always had liars among us and people promised what they thought they had to in order to get what they wanted from us. Politicians didn't invent that. But the empty promises that appears to be on the increase in recent years has made too many people a little skeptical even of God's promises. We might not say that out loud, but we live as though His faithfulness to His word may be in doubt. Heaven and earth will cease to be before one of God's promises could fail.

FATHER, give me the will to abandon myself to Your guidance and care this day. Amen

---

Thou Thyself hast taught me — Psa. 119:102

Each of us is rightly grateful to those teachers who have, over the years of our life, opened the deep recesses of our minds to new worlds of thought and imagination. They have challenged us and inspired us to higher levels of understanding and living. They have informed us with ideas and information from both past and present and in doing so have prepared us for facing the future. But they have been mere instruments of the real Teacher. It is God who knows all things and who knows us as well. The Fountain of all knowledge and all love invites us to plunge in and satisfy our soul.

FATHER, remind me that I can never learn from You too much for may own good. Amen

---

Thy testimonies ... are the joy of my heart
— Psa. 119:111

Young lovers separated by great distances may talk on the phone for hours and feel for a moment that the miles have slipped away. But a letter from that loved one is different from what has been said in the past. Words on paper have a kind of staying power lacked by the spoken word. They can be read again and again in special times, indeed at any time. Each word and phrase can be studied over and savored. Such are the words of Scripture for believers. They speak of God's love in countless ways and seemingly in fresh ways each time we read them.

FATHER, speak to me of Your love again as I read the message from Your heart in Your word today. Amen

---

Thou art my hiding place and my shield
— Psa. 119:114

Each one of us has those times in life when we need a place to go and let the wounds of life have time to heal. This retreat does not mean that we have abandoned the battle that rages continually around us. However, it does signify that we must rest and be restored so that we can again engage the enemy. All the while, the One who really wages war on behalf of our soul does not slack in the fight. He continues alone until we are once again able to stand beside Him. When we are able, He expects us to again take up His shield and join Him in the march to victory.

FATHER, do not let me linger so long in healing my wounds that I become comfortable in that safety You have provided. Amen

---

Deal with Thy servant according to Thy
lovingkindness
— Psa. 119:124

Most of us are basically good folks. We have not and will not break any major law. We don't even understand what goes on in the mind of someone who continually flaunts the law as though it does not apply to them. We are inclined to keep the laws of our society. We are even inclined to keep the laws of God. But we do fail in that too. We stand guilty before God. Yet He does not want retribution because He loves us. If He were to go strictly by His own law and give us what we deserve we would be lost. But in Jesus Christ He has offered us His mercy loving-kindness. Still some reject the offer to their own damnation.

FATHER, I cling to Your mercy as my only hope of salvation. Amen

---

Establish my footsteps in Thy word — Psa. 119:133

For many, if not most believers, the Bible is such a revered book that it is seldom read. We claim to believe the Bible and often attach special words to describe how much we believe about it and yet its claim on our life is much more difficult to see. What we really believe in is what guides our life from day to day. What we say we trust demands a lingering thought from time to time but is not what gives direction in the circumstances of daily life. IF the Scriptures contain any word from God to mankind, that word must be the underpinning of all that we do and are.

FATHER, I accept Your direction for my life from Your word today. Amen

---

Righteous art Thou, O Lord — Psa. 119:137

"It's just not fair!" How many times we utter those words when things in life go wrong. We look for "a break," or better luck, or different circumstances, or anything else that would make our lives better as we believe we deserve. We blame politicians or anyone else we don't like anyway. We may even blame God for our troubles. But it is God who is at work in all our circumstances bringing about good to those who love Him. God is not required to do something that pleases us in order to be good. Everything God does is good and righteous because He is what righteousness is.

FATHER, I give You praise today because You are whatever is good in my circumstances and my life. Amen

----

I wait for Thy words — Psa. 119:147

WAIT? It seems we spend an inordinate amount of each day just waiting for someone or something. Much of the waiting is an aggravation because we look on it as such a waste of our time. But when we are waiting for someone special we might use the delay to better prepare ourselves for the meeting. Such a waiting time can heighten our awareness and appreciation to the point that when the person arrives we are at our peak for the rendezvous What a marvelous experience is ours when we prepare ourselves with prayer to meet God in His word!

FATHER, I wait almost breathlessly for each meeting with You today in prayer and the reading of Your word. Amen

----

Great are Thy mercies, O Lord — Psa. 119:156

Most of us have had occasion to stand with mouth agape as we have viewed one of the so-called natural wonders of our world. We also marvel at some of the achievements of humanity. We stand in awe of those who have overcome incredible obstacles to reach their goals. And yet we often take the works of God in our own life for granted. But how can we cease to wonder at the compassion of our heavenly Father? How is it possible to be the recipient of such mercy and not be overwhelmed continually? That mercy binds us forever in love and gratitude. What other response could we have?

FATHER, thank you for being merciful to me, a sinner. Amen

My heart stands in awe of Thy words
— Psa. 119:161

One of the continuing marvels of Scripture to anyone who reads them with a prayerful heart is that their message is always fresh. Though many have studied it seeking to plumb its depths for a lifetime yet they always declare that still more remains. Even the casual reader of the Bible, as most of us are, has found that when we turn to it in time of confusion or distress we have found a word that has spoken to our situation. What we discover is that it is not the words of the Bible that have the most important thing to say. Rather it is the way God has of speaking through the words to our need.

FATHER, help me to truly revere the Scriptures by putting them into practice in my life today. Amen

---

Let my tongue sing of Thy word — Psa. 119:172

Thankfully, ours is a singing faith. The Bible demonstrates for us that our faith can sing regardless of the circumstances. It records for all time the songs of deepest sorrow and the songs of highest joy. The Scriptures lead us in songs of triumph and defeat. And yet in all these songs is praise for our heavenly Father. Through all the storms of life our songs give thanks to Him for He leads us on and even carries us when that is needed. In the celebrations of victory and joy He is One who deserves and receives praise. We learn of these songs of earlier times from the Bible and we overflow with praise because God has preserved His message in it.

FATHER, cause my heart to continue rejoicing because of Your word. Amen

---

In my trouble I cried to the Lord — Psa. 120:1

How often it is true of us that we call on the Lord most when we are in trouble. We are aware in those times that we need Him. But most of our days we don't think much about God. He is the One who takes care of problems. As long as our life is going well we seem to feel little need for the One who gave us life, the One who gives us health, the One who gives us all the things we have. And though many might call us ingrates for taking God's goodness to us for granted, He still hears our prayers when we realize we need Him.

FATHER, because You hear me in my trouble I will call on You also just when I want to enjoy Your nearness. Amen

---

He that keeps you will not slumber — Psa. 121:3

When we are protected by electrical or mechanical contraptions we may wonder from time to time if they will perform correctly when they are needed. When some person is given the responsibility of ensuring our safety we may have concern that they are awake and on the job. But our heavenly Father is absolutely dependable. He is watching over us at all times. He does not desert His post under the fire of the enemy and He does not weary in His care for His children. He will not fail to preserve those who love Him.

FATHER, help me to trust You enough to abandon myself to Your care. Amen

---

For the sake of the house of the Lord — Psa. 122:9

Motives may ruin even the best of goals in life and can ennoble otherwise insignificant aims. Searching out our reasons for doing things can give us a greater understanding of ourselves. What can really humble us is when we honestly admit our motives for doing our church work or our service to God. Are we seeking to earn the favor of God when we take all these church jobs on ourselves? Are we trying to appear more spiritual to our church friends? Or is our reason even more selfish in wanting power in whatever arena we can get it? None of these motives is that good. God seeks servants who will do His bidding simply for love of Him.

FATHER, I give myself to Your service today because You have already given Your best for me. Amen

---

To Thee I lift up my eyes — Psa. 123:1

We so easily get bogged down in the daily activities of life. We have so many things demanding our time and energies. Though we know it is needful, it is still difficult to take a look at a project in the long term not to mention a long view of life. What we need during these days is not just a look at our situation from the long view but an upward look at our heavenly Father. When we are feeling so dragged down we need to lift our hearts to God. When life in the "trenches" has caused us to lose our vision we need to raise our vision to God.

FATHER, in the midst of my routine today catch my eye so that I may see my job and my world differently. Amen

---

Had it not been the Lord who was on our side
— Psa. 124:2

Few of us like to take on difficulties on our own. We prefer to have as many friends and allies in the effort as we can muster. We seek support from those who have traveled that way before and are aware of particular hazards to be faced. We enlist those who we know to have been helpers and encouragers in the past. But in spite of the obvious help all these can be at various times, we need our heavenly Father with us. He alone knows all the hazards we will encounter. Only He can be the encourager and counselor we need in those dark hours of trouble.

FATHER, thank You for allowing me to know Your presence regardless of the difficulties I may face today. Amen

---

The Lord surrounds His people — Psa. 125:2

We are constantly in the midst of hostile territory in this world. The forces of evil are on the attack against all of God's creation. Most people on the earth are hapless victims of the destroyer Satan. His fiery darts and arrows are just as surely aimed in the direction of God's chosen ones. They may nick us on occasion or even deal us painful wounds. But they cannot annihilate even one of God's own. He has promised to go with us wherever we may go in His service. His power is with Him and in His presence we will not be defeated. His presence will bear us safely through to His glorious eternity.

FATHER, I trust myself to Your presence to strengthen and carry me through this day for You. Amen

---

The Lord has done great things for us — Psa. 126:3

Sometimes in the midst of some difficulty we get our attention so focused on our problem that we can only see that. During a time of trial we are not interested in what God did at some time in the past. Some even have the notion that God is either not paying attention to their hardship or maybe doesn't care any longer. At heart we really know better. If we can ever stop focusing on the problem long enough to seek the presence of God we remember. Each time we have been through some valley of shadows we have seen His goodness again in even more powerful ways. Then we remember and are strengthened for the battles ahead.

FATHER, I feel Your power in me growing as I turn my thoughts toward Your goodness. Amen

---

Unless the Lord builds the house — Psa. 127:1

In recent years there has been a lot of discussion on the subject of "Who's in charge?" This question has been around for centuries, if not millennia. Wars have been fought over it and families have been divided over it. Laws have been passed and sometimes doctrinal statements have been issued to clarify it. Still many feel that they are being subjugated and are resentful. Part of the reason for the ill-feeling is the fact that all who assume headship make their own share of mistakes. They are all, in the end, fallible human beings. True headship must always be in the hands of God. He does not delegate this job to any one of us.

FATHER, I yield myself to Your lordship in all matters today. Amen

---

Blessed is everyone ... who walks in His ways
— Psa. 128:1

We all seem to have the habit of placing people into categories. The practice does make it easier for us to deal with people rather than dealing with individual persons. But God's grace, even though it is extended to "whosoever," is still custom-made for each person. His blessing is on each one of us who is willing to live according to the way He made us. And on our side we understand that such a way of life is a blessing in itself. Far from being a crimp in our style, the way of God is the way to fullness and rightness of life.

FATHER, guide me into Your ways today so that I may enjoy the abundant life for which You made me. Amen

---

We bless you in the name of the Lord — Psa. 129:8

It is so easy in these days to emphasize the things that divide us. The tragedy is that focusing on those things brings about a negative attitude toward those people who are different or have differing views. We may find ourselves speaking in almost hateful terms against those engaged in activities we believe to be against our values. We cannot expect a sinner to behave as though he is not one. Neither should we get rankled by a lost world that rejects our lifestyle. Rather than calling down fire from heaven on unbelievers we should be pleading for the blessing of God to come to them in redemption.

FATHER, give me a loving heart toward those who are not lovable, remembering that You loved me even when I was rejecting You. Amen

---

In His word do I hope — Psa. 130:5

Promises! Promises! We have all been on the receiving end of many of them. Sadly many of them were not kept. This has made a lot of us somewhat skeptical of promises because we fear we will only be disappointed again. Some have even become skeptical of some of the promises of God. Many of His promises would indeed be hard to swallow if they were made by anyone else. But not one pledge of God has failed. He can be trusted to bring to pass every thing He has said though to the natural mind it may seem impossible. And when our hope is in His promises it is as sure as if it had already happened.

FATHER, because my hope is in You, I have no room for fear of my future. Amen

---

O Lord, my heart is not proud, nor my eyes haughty — Psa. 131:1

From the beginning of our lives we are taught to think well of ourselves. We learn that one of the keys to a happy life is good self-esteem. What we don't learn is that it's just a small step from good self-esteem to unfounded pride. For many pride is easily acquired because family and friends. In our competitive society we feel it necessary to promote ourselves and our abilities not just as being good but as being better than someone else's. That pride can then lead us to feeling invulnerable. We must take special care that we not extend this attitude toward God. Humility is the only attitude by which we may approach God.

FATHER, I lay all my achievements and goodness aside as I come to You today. Amen

———————

Let us worship at His footstool — Psa. 132:7

What a gracious invitation God has extended to all who love Him! What a privilege we have to come into His presence and humble ourselves before the heavenly Father! What an awe-full thing to know that the Holy One is near! Our question need not be what He would do if He were in our place but whether what we are doing is worthy of Him. Surely He deserves our praise and worship. He is entitled to our best. The One who sacrificed Himself for our redemption is worthy of all that we have and are. Just as surely our highest place is prostrate at His feet.

FATHER, again today I willingly place all I am and have at Your feet. Amen

———————

How good and how pleasant ...
to dwell together in unity!
— Psa. 133:1

How else would we know this if we had not read it in the pages of Scripture? Mankind has been at odds since shortly after the second person was introduced into the creation. Siblings have argued, families have divided, communities have chosen sides, and nations have taken up arms against each other. Even within the family of God an occasional fractious spirit undermines attempts at unity. Maybe this is why the psalmist speaks so wistfully and a little "wish-fully" about unity. Perhaps, like you, he saw it a few times when God's Spirit breathed like fire among His people and differences were forgotten for a time for the sake of showing the Gospel in the flesh to a world lost in sin.

FATHER, open my spirit to the spirit of others around me today so that we may labor together in the spread of the gospel. Amen

---

Lift up your hands ... and bless the Lord
— Psa. 134:1

Wait a minute! God is the One who blesses us, not the other way around. That is the way we think, isn't it? God is the giver of all things good. We are the ones who receive and sometimes give thanks. How do we go about "blessing" God? Surely there is more to blessing Him than lifting and waving our hands in excitement, as fulfilling as that may be to us in our joy. In the Old Testament, lifting one's hands was an attitude of prayer. This, then, is what blesses God. He is blessed by our desire to have fellowship with Him. Isn't that interesting? What blesses us most is also that which brings a blessing to God.

FATHER, I am again amazed that my time with You should also be a special time for You. Amen

---

Whatever the Lord pleases, He does — Psa. 135:6

If this were said about anyone but the God and Father of us all, it might make Him sound capricious or even dangerous. We certainly know what we would be like if we could each do as we pleased. All of us have known such spoiled brats of all ages. But to know that God does as He pleases can be a great comfort to each of us. Our heavenly Father is not pushed into doing anything against His will. Both His redemption of us and His judgment of us come from the same heart that loves us eternally. God wants to cleanse all of His creation and make it whole again and He is at work on that at all times.

FATHER, I am thankful that You are at work in me to bring about Your good pleasure. Amen

---

His lovingkindness is everlasting — Psa. 136:1

Just listen to our talk after learning of someone we know has done something wrong. Most of us are willing to put the error aside and give that person another chance. But hear us after learning of some crime committed by a stranger against one of ours and there is less talk about leniency or mercy. Tune in when we have heard about some heinous crime committed against anyone and we most often insist on the maximum punishment. But God, because of the great love He has for us, is rich in mercy even to those who oppose Him to the last. God's mercy is not strained as it reaches out to the worst of us with the love and mercy He has for each of us.

FATHER, remind me of my own need for Your loving-kindness even when I may think I am good. Amen

---

We sat down and wept, when we remembered
— Psa. 137:1

How long has it been since you took a hard and honest look at your own sinfulness? Your sins may be little things that trip you up in your daily walk. It is so easy to feel some brief guilt and then push it from your mind. Or your sins may be bigger things in which you indulge yourself on occasion. The guilt from these may be more long term. But see them for a moment in terms of the pain they bring to the heart of God. Like any form of infidelity they tear at the cords of the relationship. Any injury to our relationship with God must cause us grief. God longs to mend the damage done through His love and our repentance so that joy may be ours once again.

FATHER, cleanse me from the sins that threaten to weaken the bond I want with You today. Amen

On the day I called Thou didst answer me
— Psa. 138:3

Too often we use God as a last resort. We try to solve our problem on our own. When we fail, we turn to friends, or professionals, or anyone else who might be of assistance. After we have exhausted almost all the other options the eternal truth suddenly dawns on us. We know God can help us and yet we refuse to ask Him. When we do we discover that He was prepared from the beginning to come to our aid. But He will not force Himself on us. However, when we recognize our need of Him we find that He is not only able but willing to deliver us.

FATHER, forgive me for wasting our time by turning to anyone else but You. Amen

---

Such knowledge is too wonderful for me
— Psa. 139:6

Speechless! Have you ever stopped in the middle of reading some portion of the Scriptures so overwhelmed with what you just saw that your mind simply could not comprehend it? One story after another chronicles the many ways in which God has shown His love for His people. Promise after promise reveals His continuing care for His loved ones. With each one our jaw drops in amazement at His plans for His own. Because of these things the reading of the Bible becomes a tireless venture for one whose heart and mind are in the reading. The old words become a new letter of His love each time we pore over those pages.

FATHER, I have found it true again today in just this brief passage and have been humbled another time by Your care for me. Amen

---

I know that the Lord will maintain the cause of the afflicted — Psa. 140:12

We are usually so flighty in our concern. We become aware of needs and worry about them or even do something about them for a while. But our compassion seems to wear thin rather quickly. Few things seem to hold our attention for very long, then we are ready to move on to some new problem. But God keeps caring. Through good times and bad He keeps loving us and caring about our situation. Our problems are never too big or too small for His concern. God keeps on caring even over the long term. He does not become bored or disinterested with any of us. His mercy is indeed everlasting.

FATHER, I thank You for being a part of my world today. Amen

Set a guard, O Lord, over my mouth — Psa. 141:3

Most of us have had the experience expressed in the adage about putting our tongue in motion before putting our brain in gear. Just as bad, if not worse, is the verbalizing of some of our thoughts. Some of the ideas that run through our mind are best kept away from any human ears. It is in the recesses of our minds that we hopefully give due consideration to those things that we will speak. It is in that mind that we determine the value of what we think to say and whether it is worthy. It is in that thought process that we desperately need the tempering of our words by the Spirit of God. Here is the importance of being "slow to speak."

FATHER, may the words of my mouth and the thoughts of my heart today be that which is acceptable to You. Amen

---

Thou wilt deal bountifully with me — Psa. 142:7

We look with horror and disgust on parents who willingly withhold the necessities of life from their children. We even show some disdain for moms and dads who are unwilling to sacrifice in order to provide the best they can for their kids. Why is it that we would think our heavenly Father is so grudging with His provisions for us? We often pray as though He must be persuaded with tears to do what is good for us. We would loathe such an earthly father. Surely our God in heaven always wants the very best for His children. We can be confident that He will provide even more than we think or ask.

FATHER, because of You I know that I shall not lack any good thing. Amen

---

Teach me to do Thy will — Psa. 143:10

As children most of us took many years to get into the practice of knowing and doing the will of our parents. But as we mature we come to understand the intent of our parents and the wisdom behind some of the rules by which we were supposed to live. Doing the will of our heavenly Father also requires time and maturity in the faith. As we grow in Him He guides us in the ways He would have us go. We find that the time we spend with Him teaches us His ways and the joy of walking in them.

FATHER, I submit myself to Your will and ways today that my joy may be made full. Amen

---

I will sing a new song to Thee, O God — Psa. 144:9

Music, I suppose, is one of the greatest achievements of human kind. It has given us an avenue of expression that goes beyond words to express the thoughts the soul is unable to communicate in any other way. Songs enable us to bring forth from the depths the longings, the disappointments, a whole range of emotions that otherwise would languish there and leave the heart empty. But the heart that has known the presence of God in redemption simply MUST sing. The experience of His mercy is too wonderful for mere words. It requires music so that our souls can soar nearer to the realms to which He is leading us.

FATHER, Your love is truly the "theme of my song" today. Amen

---

His mercies are over all His works — Psa. 145:9

We must stand in awe at the fact that the Creator of the universe is willing to stay involved in His handiwork. Surely the whole thing has become flawed because of the sin of mankind. Yet God is more than Creator. He is Sustainer. He is Father. As Father He could not watch idly as we have spoiled His work. Neither could He as Father bear to destroy those who have brought sin into His world. As Father He continues to reach out for us in His mercy to restore us and all of His works to what they could be.

FATHER, help me to receive even Your chastening as Your mercy upon me. Amen

---

The Lord sets the prisoners free — Psa. 146:7

We began serving time quite early in life. We cannot really complain about the sentence because we committed the crime by our own choosing. The early years of our confinement was little different from before. We still had most of our freedoms and hardly noticed the walls and, frankly, didn't care. The apparent laxness of our jailer lulled us into letting our freedom slowly ebb away. One day we awoke to find ourselves hopelessly and mercilessly confined. Our own sin did this to each of us. But our heavenly Father who loves us beyond our imagining has the keys!

FATHER, help me to live gratefully today as one who has been set free. Amen

---

He heals the brokenhearted and binds
up their wounds — Psa. 147:3

Being sick, no matter the ailment, can be a lonely and frightening time especially when you are not sure of the cause or cure. Others may offer suggestions for remedies whose effectiveness we may doubt or see as the only straw to which we can cling. The one cure for our sickness of sin is truly incredible. That is the grace of the God whom our sin has most grievously offended. Our heavenly Father alone has the power to heal us and the self-sacrificing commitment to making us whole. Even daily He continues to cleanse the cuts and scrapes of sin from His children and to wipe away the tears we have brought on ourselves.

FATHER, when I fall down because of my sin I give You thanks that You bring healing to me again. Amen

---

His name alone is exalted — Psa. 148:13

Who gets the credit for who or what you are? If things have turned out badly in our life we usually are anxious to find someone on whom we can pin the blame. However, there are many who are more than willing to take all the credit for their own success. If we do give that honor to someone else it is often some guru who wrote a book that gave us the motivation or information to make it big. But if there is anything good about us we must understand that it is from God. If we have done anything truly good it will bring glory to God. If we have achieved or become anything worthwhile it has been through the power of God working in us. All glory is due to Him.

FATHER, may Your name be exalted through everything I choose to do today. Amen

---

The Lord takes pleasure in His people — Psa. 149:4

Parental pride is normal and heart-warming to observe in a young couple with small children. They are convinced that their children are at the very top of every list of superlatives. But what of the parents of children who have gone wrong? Is it pride or shame they feel as they watch their children go against everything they have been taught? What does it do to the heart of God when each one of His goes wrong? He does not love His wayward children any less than those who have returned to His paths. But God takes special delight in His children who continue in His ways.

Father, may my thoughts and actions today bring pleasure to Your heart. Amen

———————

Let everything that has breath praise the Lord
— Psa. 150:6

What a way to sum up a book of prayer and praise! This is the total duty of human kind. Nothing else we might think to do as a believer comes close to this obligation. All the works we do should point to and give glory and praise to God. The very thoughts of our hearts should be such as give honor to His name. This is not just true for believers. The Scriptures teach us that one day "every knee shall bow and every tongue confess." The Bible also indicates that the great benediction at the close of time and the constant hymn throughout eternity will be words of praise to God.

Father, may the words of my mouth and the thoughts of my heart be a ceaseless praise of You. Amen

———————

PROVERBS

Savoring God's Wisdom

A wise man will hear — Prov. 1:5

For many of us the practice of listening to someone is very difficult. We have so much that we want to say. Even when we are not speaking we are often planning what we will say next rather than listening. Prayer, which is supposed to be a time of communication with God, rarely consists of more than our side of the conversation. Study of the Scriptures becomes a search for words that will make us feel better or confirm our opinions rather than an opportunity to be still and let the Word speak its message to us from God. If we are truly wise we will listen far more than we speak. Then we will be able to hear.

FATHER, keep the ears of my heart tuned to hear Your voice in the midst of my circumstances today. Amen

---

You ... did not want my reproof — Prov. 1:25

No one really wants to be told they have done something wrong. Instead, we are usually so proud of what we have accomplished or attempted that it's hard for us to believe that anyone could have a different opinion. Accepting criticism or correction requires an admission that your pride and joy needs some improvement. Only when we have obviously and miserably failed are we willing to readily receive correction. The trouble is that our view of our work is distorted by pride. It often takes a less involved person to show us the flaws. More importantly, it takes the viewpoint of our Father who is intimately involved to show us our true shortcomings and give us His unerring guidance into the right way.

FATHER, open my eyes and ears to Your judgment on my life today. Amen

---

The complacency of fools shall destroy them — Prov. 1:32

It is one thing to be in danger without being aware of it. It is altogether another matter to be in danger and ignore the fact. Deliberately ignoring our circumstances might give us some peace of mind and might even masquerade itself as faith. "Leaving it to God" can be a cop-out for an unwillingness to tackle a situation. This kind of "hands off" approach can be deadly. God wants us to be aware of our circumstances and also to be aware of His power over our circumstances. He also wants us to be aware that His power in us can face the challenge of any danger and overcome it.

FATHER, I willingly face up to my circumstances today with the wisdom and power that come from You. Amen

---

The Lord gives wisdom — Prov. 2:6

In this information age isn't it striking that there should be such a lack of wisdom. Even among those we would consider highly intelligent we find such foolish behavior. We have seemingly lost sight of the difference between having information and having wisdom. The Bible exhorts us to get wisdom along with our knowledge. The ability to employ any body of knowledge in an effective and productive manner is a gift from God. He offers His wisdom to any who lacks it. Only with His wisdom can we hope to tackle the circumstances of life in these days.

FATHER, I ask for Your wisdom which I must have to make it through the obstacle course of this day. Amen

---

Keep to the paths of the righteous — Prov. 2:20

We would all do much better in life it seems if we didn't have so many choices. Depending somewhat on where you live the options each day are almost limitless. Deep in our hearts we believers know that it is always best to stay on the path God has set for us. However, our real challenge is to discern which of the often similar paths is the right one. Much of the sin we wander into is not directly opposed to what is right, but is a slightly lesser substitute. We cannot assume that just because it looks good that it is right. We must constantly seek His face as our guide.

FATHER, turn me from the lesser paths into Your strait and narrow way. Amen

---

Let your heart keep My commandments – Prov. 3:1

We all know that God has issued commandments by which we are to pattern our lives. We also know that God has the right to demand anything from His creatures. For that reason we may feel constrained to keep them because we realize He has the power to punish us if we don't. But God is not interested in breathing robots who follow His commands without a thought. Neither does He desire slaves to obey His wishes out of fear of punishment. Instead, He wants followers who love Him and who obey Him from a heart overflowing with thankfulness.

FATHER, I yield myself to Your perfect desire for my life today. Amen

---

Honor the Lord from your wealth — Prov. 3:9

All of us who have been around the church for very long have heard about stewardship. Most of what we hear is about the responsibility to give a tithe of our income to the church. What we hear much less about is our responsibility before God for the portion of our income that we keep for our own use. As with our lives so with our other resources, we must honor God with all of them or we bring Him no honor at all. Nothing less than our best is sufficient for what God means to us.

FATHER, such as I have I give to You today. Amen

The Lord will be your confidence — Prov. 3:26

Many folks have become quite cynical in these days because of promises made and broken by individuals and institutions. Some solve the problem by refusing to trust anyone. That may keep you safe but it will also keep you very lonely. In spite of the fact that there are certain risks involved each of us needs someone we can trust. But whom can we trust? Only one person we know has a proven record of trustworthiness. Only our heavenly Father has consistently carried through on every promise. And because of

His great love for us we can be certain that He never will.

FATHER, I unquestioningly place myself into Your loving care today. Amen

---

Do not withhold good — Prov. 3:27

Among those who have more financial resources than most of us, helping persons who are in need is usually referred to as charity. They often give large sums with great fanfare perhaps because it helps their image. Those of us with lesser reserves make donations to helping organizations who pool our money with donations from others to do a lot of good. After we've made these contributions from what we have to spare we often turn a deaf ear to other needs around us. How can we remain rather comfortably secluded and close our eyes and ears to the reminder of "There but for the grace of God . . . ?"

FATHER, help me not to become so attached to my lifestyle that I will not hear the cries of need around me. Amen

---

He is intimate with the upright — Prov. 3:32

We share ourselves with people on different levels. Our acquaintances know us only on a very superficial level. Our co-workers are familiar with us on a different level. Our friends know us in a somewhat deeper dimension. However, most of us are truly intimate with only a small number of people if any at all. We may still have secrets from our spouse or closest friends, but none from Him. And, best of all, He does not withhold Himself from us. To those who are willing to walk closely with Him, the Father reveals all of Himself we can possibly handle. We must decide how close we want to be with Him.

FATHER, keep me mindful that the barriers to our intimacy have all been set up by me. Amen

---

Keep My commandments and live — Prov. 4:4

Most of us go through stages in our lives when we rebel against the rules and question the right of those in authority. We spend at least a portion of our lives trying to blaze new trails, wanting to do it our own way. Our own way never works, though. Some of us learn that lesson quickly; but most of us continue to try to break out on occasion throughout our lives. We always discover, later rather than sooner, that the path God sets before all His children is the best way for us to go. Like young adults who suddenly discover how smart their parents were all along, we learn that God's way makes us the best we can be.

FATHER, when I bolt from Your path, draw me quickly back for my own good. Amen

---

Do not enter the path of the wicked — Prov. 4:14

It is perhaps within the nature of the human animal to be curious about those things outside our personal experience. In a young child we see this as part of growing and developing. Even in an adult it is properly viewed as broadening one's understanding of the world around him. But also a part of our fallen nature is the desire to experiment with those types of behavior that morality in general and the Bible in particular warn us against. Dabbling of this sort can be fatal for the believer's witness and can be injurious to his relationship with God. Even when we are considering evil we are building a wall between ourselves and the Father.

FATHER, my desire is to cling to Your hand so that I do not wander from Your side. Amen

---

Watch over your heart with all diligence
– Prov. 4:23

Too many of us seem to have the notion that our behavior after we become believers is on automatic pilot. It is as though we believe that since we are now the children of God we no longer have to make decisions about the right paths to choose. The stark reality is that even when we know the right way we should go we still face the often tough decision to go in that right way. The attacks of the Deceiver come more often and with more intensity as we draw closer to the heavenly Father. The good news is that as Satan's attacks are growing stronger, we are drawing closer to the Father. His strength is added to our strength to defeat the temptations as they come.

FATHER, I know that I will be in a struggle with sin today, but I thank You for the assurance that I will not be alone in it. Amen

---

She does not ponder the path of life — Prov. 5:6

Taking life one day at a time has become a very popular idea in these times. The pace of life is so hectic and some of its problems can overwhelm us when we try to take it all in at once. But this must not discourage us from giving some thought to the future. Without at least some thinking about the future we can have no sense of direction and could spend our lives going in circles. For the believer, there is a goal and it is not just heaven. That is our destination and that is in God's hands. But the goal of our life is to bring honor and glory to God. That does not happen automatically.

FATHER, do not allow me to become so absorbed in today that I lose sight of my mission for You with my whole life. Amen

---

I was almost in utter ruin — Prov. 5:14

Most of us have a difficult time seeing the desperation of the situation of our lives before we became a Christian. We were reared in nice families, most of whom went to church. We grew up as not-too-terrible children and teens. Though we were not angelic, still the mischief we got into and the trouble we caused our parents was probably the normal stuff and little more. "Utter ruin" would appear to be a gross over-statement of our predicament. And yet before we came to Jesus we were each destined for the ultimate ruin of hell itself. When we recall what may have been a subtle change in our lives when we became a Christian we must also think for a moment on the fact that we were snatched from the pathway to eternal damnation.

FATHER, I thank You for having mercy on a doomed sinner like me. Amen

---

He will be held with the cords of his sin
— Prov. 5:22

Surely all of us have been told about "the tangled web" spun by attempts to deceive. Even if we were not warned about it we have learned from the experience of trying to cover up earlier lies. But the web is bigger than the trap of deception. Though spiders, the master web-spinners, are never caught in their own devices, the web of sin always snares the one who wove it. With each sinful thought and act we become more tightly entwined until we are totally at the mercilessness of the one who taught us to spin. This web of sin can only be broken by the matchless mercy of Him who loves us.

FATHER, loose me from the strands of sin that, in my weakness, I may spin today. Amen

---

You have been snared with the words of your mouth
— Prov. 6:2

The Bible warns us about the potential of our tongue for destroying our life. We have all had some experience with rumors and gossip and "little white lies." Whether receiving or sending such malicious and destructive words, each of us has felt some of the pain they can cause. In these days of the increase of printed words on a geometric scale, the spoken word has been somewhat devalued. But written and electronic documents may be destroyed or even ignored. Words spoken, however, can never be erased or destroyed. They are passed on from hearer to hearer, continually building up or tearing down.

FATHER, remind me of the long-term effect of each word I utter today. Amen

---

Reproofs for discipline are the way of life
— Prov. 6:23

None of us like criticism. Even when it's construc-
tive we are hardly able to avoid seeing it as a put
down. As children we might have been able to see
it as a necessary step in growing up. We either willingly accepted it, or at least endured it, until we were
grown up and could tell others what to do. But we
never get beyond the need for discipline unless we
view discipline only as punishment. We still have
need of direction from those who have more intimate
knowledge of certain aspects of our daily journey in
life. We have not been precisely in this place before
and we need the guidance of the One who has.

FATHER, I look to You for the discipline I will need to
negotiate my way through this new territory called
Today. Amen

———————

He who would destroy himself does it — Prov. 6:32

A person who deliberately drinks a deadly poison
should not be surprised when he dies from it. One
who jumps in front of a high speed train should not be
disappointed that he is killed. Some kinds of behavior
naturally bring destruction. No one can presume to
play fast and loose with life and escape unharmed.
Having the money or the power or the opportunity
to hide this behavior from the sight of others does
not exempt us from the destruction which is going

on in the heart all the while. "May I do it" and "Can I do it" are not nearly so important as "Should I do it." The road to destruction is broad and inviting, but the narrow way to life is still found by some to their great joy.

FATHER, I long to walk in Your way because this life eternal. Amen

---

Keep ... my teaching as the apple of your eye
— Prov. 7:2

Elsewhere in the Scriptures God speaks of Israel being the apple of His eye. That is an expression that leads us to understand the supreme value placed by God on Israel. We are encouraged to place that sort of importance on His teachings. This also means that we keep His instructions at the very center of our focus as we go through life. Instead of relegating God and the Bible to a supporting role or on the fringes of our daily lives, we are to keep our minds on them so that we are not tempted to stray.

FATHER, help me to lift my gaze to the lofty level of the desires of Your heart for me today. Amen

---

He does not know that it will cost him his life
— Prov. 7:23

Hardly a week passes without some new revelation in the media about something we are eating or otherwise using that is dangerous to our health. Most of us have a brief scare and then go on with our lives as before. When we have had fair warning and still walk head-long into death we rightly garner little sympathy. But the great tragedy all around us each day is the large number of people hurtling ever closer to an eternal dying in the fires of hell because they do not know. Can we be bystanders to such needless destruction when we hold the key to the door of life?

FATHER, burden my soul with the needless tragedy of some around me dying without Christ. Amen

---

Wisdom is better than jewels — Prov. 8:11

Many in our day misunderstand wisdom as meaning a collection of knowledge or information. But the biblical term is nearer to that uncommon quality we know as "common sense." Rather than mere knowledge, this is the ability to use knowledge in the best possible way. Without this common sense we allow very valuable things and ideas to slip past us while searching for that bauble or trinket we are convinced will satisfy us. This is that same wisdom the Scriptures teach us that God is so eager to give us and yet so many of us still are lacking because we have filled our prayers with requests for lesser things.

FATHER, teach me to seek Your wisdom before all other desires of my heart. Amen

---

He marked out the foundations of the earth
— Prov. 8:29

In this scientific age when theories are put forth to explain how things have come to be, we believers are forced to decide where God's hand fits into the origin of these things. For some of us it is a simple matter of accepting the reasoned speculations of the scientific community and removing those things from the category explained by God. For still others of us it is a continuing defensive struggle to hold on to some explanations that include God. For some others of us there is not concern that science will explain our universe so well that we no longer have need of God. For this group there is a certainty of faith that God's fingerprints are all over creation and that His loving hands still guide it to His purposes.

FATHER, I thank You that you are always somewhat beyond anything I may ever discover but are always very near to me in Your love. Amen

---

Forsake your folly and live — Prov. 9:6

All of us would surely like to be able to "have our cake and eat it too." That is the way too many of us try to live the Christian life. We want to be known among our Christian friends as Christian, but maybe not so much so among our non-Christian friends. Many of us want to participate in worldly activities that take our minds off the things of God so that we may better fit in with the people we work with and those in our community. In short, we are much like Lot's wife. We all want to go to heaven, but we hesitate to leave behind the pleasures that would distract us. It's as though we really think those going to hell may be enjoying life more than we.

FATHER, remind me again that what I have found in You brings more joy in this life than all the pleasures of sin. Amen

---

The fear of the Lord is the beginning of wisdom
— Prov. 9:10

When did you begin your education? No matter when you began your formal schooling your learning began the instant your life began. You couldn't help but learn as you faced a new environment and had new experiences moment after moment. The older you got the more choices you had about whether you would learn. Our new birth into the family of God also brought a new environment and new experiences which caused us to learn things about our God and ourselves. But as we have grown older in the faith too many of us have chosen not to learn and grow. Deliberate spiritual ignorance is the worst kind of folly.

FATHER, keep my eyes open and my heart yearning to know You better so that I may serve You more completely. Amen

---

The memory of the righteous is blessed
— Prov. 10:7

Each of us wants to leave something behind for others to remember. Writers and other artists are often practically unknown until after they have died. Great rulers in early times erected enormous and expensive monuments to themselves during their reign. But few can manage to have a lasting impact on the world. The most that the majority of us can do is hope that someone will remember us. The good news is that no matter how insignificant we may feel we are in the grand scheme of things, as a child of God we are remembered by Him with His blessing.

FATHER, I thank You that even in my lowest valleys I can count on being important to You. Amen

---

He who walks in integrity walks securely
— Prov. 10:9

Living a lie is like walking around in a mine field. With each safe step you take you can feel some relief but you have to realize that it's only temporary. Usually each act or word of deceit demands another. Each attempt to mislead leads to a further entanglement. You must have a good memory to continue down the path of lies. Living truthfully avoids the dangerous way of deceit. Walking with integrity means that you need not worry about secrets being revealed, behavior being exposed, or conversations being repeated.

FATHER, guide me in my living today so that I have no need to fear the observations of others. Amen

---

The wages of the righteous is life — Prov. 10:16

We know from the writings of Paul that "the wages of sin is death." But we are accustomed to thinking of life as a gift from God and not as wages for good behavior. The solution to this is, of course, rather simple. If we could be righteous we would deserve to have everlasting life as wages. But the same Bible tells us that there is, in fact, no one who is righteous on his own. Our heavenly Father is the one who, through His marvelous grace, makes us righteous through the work of Christ. The natural consequences of that imputed righteousness is that we receive life everlasting and life in abundance even now.

FATHER, thank You for Your gift of righteousness and the consequent life that has become mine. Amen

---

The lips of the righteous feed many — Prov. 10:21

The Scriptures warn us about the dangers of the human tongue. Often we are cautioned in its pages of dire consequences of words spoken in anger or without thought. But the Bible also encourages the believer to speak encouragement and right instruction to those who, for the moment at least, are weak. We cannot know how often the right word can life someone who might have decided that life is not worth living. We may never know the lives we influence in a positive way by lives that are consistent with our words. What effect will the words you speak today have on those who hear?

FATHER, may my words and even my thoughts be uplifting to those around me today. Amen

---

The righteous has an everlasting foundation
— Prov. 10:25

It has seemed to many that in recent years we have had increasing natural disasters both in number and ferocity. Some have even seen these things as signs that the Lord's return is drawing near. Others have watched as economies around the world, including our own, have taken serious down turns and wondered if everything were collapsing. Some have looked at the upheavals in government and society in general and gotten the feeling that all we value in society is fading away. But through all of this the faithful are encouraged because their lives and their future are built on a hope that is not shaken by circumstances because it is built on the solid Rock who is Christ the Lord.

FATHER, my heart's desire is for all mankind to share this foundation which is faith in You. Amen

---

Riches do not profit in the day of wrath
— Prov. 11:4

In the last half of this last century of the millennium American culture has undergone some radical changes. We have gone from the post-war years of healing our wounded families to putting families aside for a time to make all the money we possibly can. When we have put all possible energy into acquiring more and more money and other stuff, what then? What will all this single-minded drive to amass the maximum do for us in the end? And, just as important, what is it doing to us in the meanwhile. We seem to have forgotten where the storehouse of real wealth is located. All our treasures on earth will vanish away. Only those treasures put aside in heaven will be of any value.

FATHER, help me focus on worthy goals and not worldly goals. Amen

---

He who sows righteousness gets a true reward
— Prov. 11:18

Why do you try to do what is right? Is it because you are afraid of the consequences of doing wrong? Is it because you know that the righteous will inherit eternity in heaven? Or could it be that you want to do righteousness to make the heart of your heavenly Father glad? You know how you feel when you have done something for your loved ones that they wanted or needed even if it meant great sacrifice for you. That same feeling multiplied many times is what comes from doing something for your Savior. Heaven in the future is a great reward. But the knowledge now that you have been of service to the Master may be even better.

FATHER, because of Your love and confidence in me, my desire is to please You in all that I do this day. Amen

---

The evil man will not go unpunished — Prov. 11:21

Breaking the law is, for some, a game in which the only real object seems to be to avoid getting caught for as long as possible. Others of us do really stupid things once in a while and hope no one will ever find out, but someone usually does. If nothing else, the deceit gnaws at you until you can no longer hide your actions. For a believer, the real teeth in that gnawing is the Holy Spirit convicting us of our sin. The unbeliever has that same gnawing but more easily ignores the source. He may successfully evade conviction by governmental authorities throughout his life. However, ignoring the conviction By God's Spirit will end in a final punishment by the hand of God.

FATHER, I want to stay away from sinful behavior; but when I fail I know that I must repent so that I may return to Your side. Amen

---

The desire of the righteous is only good
— Prov. 11:23

Most of us think we are being good so long as we don't DO bad things. We glare with a certain smugness at unbelievers and backsliders whose behavior goes against the clear commands of the Scriptures. We consider ourselves true to the Gospel so long as we have refrained from forbidden behavior. But think for a moment of those acts you have wished you could commit if only there were a way no one else would ever know. In addition to that which we do are even those things we want to do that indicate the kind of people we really are. Our goals and dreams for our lives must be worthy of who we claim to be.

FATHER, help me not to try to separate the thoughts and desires of my heart from who I am in You. Amen

---

The thoughts of the righteous are just — Prov. 12:5

When that crazy driver cut dangerously close in front of you this morning on your way to work, what was the first thing that crossed your mind? When you hear about some despicable behavior or some heinous crime it is easy and even "normal" to want God or someone else to vent their wrath on those who did it. We can be thankful that God does not lash out in quick judgment against our wrongdoing. If we can truly begin to love even our enemies we will discover that our "normal" reaction to attacks on us or affronts to us will be loving concern. This could be the first big step toward reconciliation.

FATHER, guard my heart and my thoughts that they may reflect Your character more than my fallen nature. Amen

---

The deeds of a man's hands will return to him
— Prov. 12:14

Sometimes we can get the mistaken impression that the work we are doing goes unnoticed. We may have been striving to help someone or just trying to do a good job, and for the moment at least our efforts may appear to be ignored. When that happens we may well become discouraged. But our Lord Jesus encourages us to continue on in our "well doing" because we will be rewarded. On the other side of the coin we must keep in mind that any unsavory behavior of ours that we hoped would be overlooked will someday return to haunt us. Even though others may never know, we can be certain as children of God that He knows and that should be deterrent enough.

FATHER, remind me that my actions and my thoughts are always in full view of the One I most want to please. Amen

———————

The tongue of the wise brings healing
— Prov. 12:18

It is true of too many of us that we often are guilty of making statements or making them in such a way that they hurt people. We might tell a partial truth that intentionally leaves a bad and wrong impression. Or we might reveal information that is not beneficial. Words can easily tear down a person's self-esteem or reputation with others. But words spoken in the right spirit can bring peace in a troubling situation. They can also serve as a vital encouragement to those who are near losing hope. How we use our words, spoken or written, reveals our heart.

FATHER, may my words today strengthen and encourage all who hear them. Amen

———————

A wise son accepts his father's discipline
— Prov. 13:1

Most of us do not like the thought of discipline, especially when applied to ourselves. One of the reasons for this is that we equate discipline with punishment. But discipline is so much more than that. Rightly conceived its meaning and purpose is to cause someone to follow a certain path. The only time punishment or pain is involved is when one deviates from the prescribed path. Our heavenly Father's discipline is like that. He graciously lets us know when we are straying from His path, not in anger but in His great love for us. When we accept His discipline we find that the "yoke" really is "easy."

FATHER, remind me today that Your path for me is not burdensome but is designed to make my life full. Amen

---

He who walks with wise men will be wise
— Prov. 13:20

We have long been told that we are known by the company we keep. What we sometimes misunderstand is that this is not just a matter of one's perception. We do not just appear to be wise because we keep company with wise people. The fact is that hobnobbing with such people has a positive effect on us and we find ourselves picking up on their attitudes and habits. We ourselves become much like them.

The bad news is that this same principle applies when our associates are less than wise. When we find ourselves associating with a bad group too much we will inevitably find ourselves picking up on their behavior as well.

FATHER, give me the wisdom to ally myself with those whose company will keep me close to You as well. Amen

---

Happy is he who is gracious to the poor
— Prov. 14:21

Being of help to someone else is perhaps the greatest privilege given to a human being. A close second to this would be the honor of being asked for help. The presentation of the request may come at a time we don't want to be bothered. It may even come from a person whose appearance or lifestyle is offensive to our sensibilities. We may spend a few moments trying to evaluate whether the person is deserving of our help. But are we capable of making this judgment? Also, haven't we been taught the blessing of being helped because of our need and not our worthiness? It is the act of helping another that brings the joy.

FATHER, because You opened Your heart to me in my desperate need, may I open my heart and my hands to the needs around me. Amen

---

The righteous has a refuge when he dies
— Prov. 14:32

Many people are attracted to the Christian faith because they see it as a safe harbor amid the swirl of trouble and danger of the modern world. Some seem to believe that once they become a believer all those problems are over and their life is one long joy-filled day until that glorious day when they go home to be with Jesus in eternal joy. But our faith does not insulate us from all the sharp edges of earthly life. The believer is even assured in Scripture that trials are a part of life. But we are also assured that our Savior has overcome the world and has made us overcomers as well. Our final triumph will be announced by that heavenly blast that will call us to our eternal home.

FATHER, I can face anything today because I am convinced that You keep me. Amen

---

Righteousness exalts a nation, but sin is a disgrace
— Prov. 14:34

Bible readers of every generation who have seen this text have had no difficulty pointing to some current event as evidence of the disgrace brought on by sin in high places. And an "everybody's done it" attitude toward sin should not diminish the embarrassment. In fact, the misdeeds of those we know bring a sense of sadness and regret to us. However, the Scriptures teach us that seeing error in another must always remind us of the sin in ourselves. And the desire to have "them" suffer the consequences must include the understanding that we stand guilty of sin ourselves. Wrongdoing must never become so common that it ceases to cause regret; but righteousness should never become so rare that it brings incredulity.

FATHER, deliver me from the sin that would bring disgrace to me and to those who know me. Amen

---

The eyes of the Lord are in every place
— Prov. 15:3

No one likes the thought of living in a fishbowl under the gaze of the whole world. Celebrities love it and hate it at the same time. They, like most of us, enjoy the attention so long as it is on their own terms. Thinking of the government as having eyes and ears everywhere can leave any of us nervous and somewhat frightened. But how are we to feel about the constant eyes of God on us? This thought will cause many of us to be much more careful about our behavior as it should. But to all of us it is also a wonderful promise. No matter how insignificant we may think ourselves to be we are never outside the watchful eye of the One who has shown His love for us at Calvary.

FATHER, I praise Your name for the promise that all my steps are within Your loving sight. Amen

---

The prayer of the upright is His delight
— Prov. 15:8

All of us can remember those times when we were
brought before our parents because we had done
something wrong. Our cheeks might even burn now
at the memory of having been caught doing something they had forbidden. We may have been somewhat frightened at the time about what they would
do to us. We were certainly embarrassed. But being
around our parents at other times was a great joy.
When we realize that we have sinned in the sight of
God it is appropriate that we feel guilty and embarrassed. But with repentance comes forgiveness and
right standing with Him. Then we have the joy of His
presence and learn that He delights in our fellowship
with Him.

FATHER, cleanse me of my sin so that I may again be
a delight to You. Amen

Before honor comes humility — Prov. 15:33

In many enterprises these days you can find a lot of
people who want to be in charge while very few seem
to want to do the real work. Young people just out
of school want to move directly into high positions
before they have the experience that would given
them wisdom for such positions. We all seem to want
the prestige and power but are much less willing to
pay the price to earn them. In our Father's house even

the greatest of persons must become again as a little child. In the Father's eyes those who are truly great are those willing to do the lowly work of the servant. In the Father's kingdom positions are not taken but are given as rewards for humble service.

FATHER, turn me from my grasping nature so that I may receive Your gifts. Amen

---

The Lord weighs the motives — Prov. 16:2

We can only judge the actions of others based on what we have seen or heard. For that reason our actions and behavior can easily be misunderstood. But there is One who does not misunderstand, who sees deep into our hearts. When others may think badly of us because of something we have done, our heavenly Father who knows our hearts is able to reassure us and comfort us. However, there is a down side to this divine knowledge. The Father also is not misled by our holy acts done for unholy reasons. Our Father always judges our actions according to the intent of our heart.

FATHER, may my actions today be unmixed with guile. Amen

The Lord has made everything for its own purpose
— Prov. 16:4

Sometimes I have wondered about that. Some of the critters that bite me or do damage to my property seem to have been accidents of God's creative process. Some of the people who live life on a sub-human level might cause you to wonder about the goodness of all of God's creation. And yet the Father continues to show me that others may at times have that view of me. When I look upon the vilest expressions of human nature I am reminded that the only thing that separates me from that is the grace of God that has given me new life through Jesus Christ. Even the vilest are still persons for whom my Lord Jesus willingly gave His life.

FATHER, deliver me again from the burden of being the judge. Amen

---

All the weights of the bag are His concern
— Prov. 16:11

Our time is so important to us that we must prioritize things so that we take care of the important matters and leave the lesser matters to someone else or leave them out altogether. Some things are just not worth bothering about. Apparently we assume that the same must be true with God. There are so many matters that could concern Him that some of them, perhaps even some people, must surely get left out. The sobering teaching of Scripture is that nothing we do escapes His notice. At the same time the glorious assurance of the Bible is that no one is so insignificant as to be beyond His care.

FATHER, remind me today that my life and the way I live it are always in Your mind. Amen

---

He who mocks the poor reproaches his Maker
— Prov. 17:5

None of us would laugh in the face of the poor. Most of us are not so far removed from that category that we would ridicule them. But as we move higher up the economic ladder there is a tendency among many to more tightly clutch their possessions to their breast. Are we afraid that those poorer ones will try to take it away? Do we hear ourselves saying that if they would work as hard as us they wouldn't be poor either? That makes them slackers who are too lazy to work and want us to support them with our tax money. Do you hear the mockery of those words? We need to remember that nothing we have of value is all of our own doing. We also need to remember that others' lack may not be all their doing either.

FATHER, as I enjoy my substance keep me mindful that it is only a stewardship intended to help others and glorify Your name. Amen

---

A rebuke goes deeper into one who has understanding — Prov. 17:10

Parents throughout history have had the experience of having their advice and admonitions to their children seem to go in one ear and out the other. Sometimes even punishment doesn't seem to get through to some folks. It seems that words of criticism or correction are often ignored or accepted as an affront. But even in children you can occasionally find one who accepts rebuke seriously and learns from it. In the same way some persons seem to chafe under the correcting words of the Scriptures. They know what the Bible teaches but convince themselves that it doesn't apply to them. But there are others whose hearts are open to the leading of God's Spirit and surely bring joy to the heart of the Father.

FATHER, may I accept Your correction, even Your discipline, with a thankful heart. Amen

------

A friend loves at all times — Prov. 17:17

Most people have a large number of acquaintances with whom they have conversations and may even share something of their personal lives. But few of those acquaintances are real friends. Friends have a deep love for each other. They expose to each other the deep thoughts and concerns of their souls. Friends are dependable, especially when you are alone in your situation. Our Lord Jesus has told His followers that He wants to be known to them as a friend. He truly is that One who can be counted on, particularly when all others may have forsaken us.

FATHER, I am thankful today that Your presence is always with me so that I am never alone. Amen

---

The name of the Lord is a strong tower
— Prov. 18:10

We take names too lightly in our culture. We often drop names of celebrities or influential people to give ourselves some of their importance. Current society encourages us to use first names in our dealing with each other. But the use of another's given name indicates a familiarity that often does not exist. The ancients understood that knowing someone's name indicated having influence with them. Our heavenly Father loves us so much that He reveals Himself to us and encourages us to "drop" the name of His Son Jesus in our conversations with Him. Knowing His name – knowing Him – is our strength.

FATHER, thank You for allowing me to know You through Jesus. Amen

---

He who finds a wife finds a good thing
— Prov. 18:22

Though much of our culture applauds the self-sufficient, none of us were created to be a solitary person. God made us incomplete from the beginning because of His desire that we find our real self in fellowship with Him and with others. That completion is seen most vividly when a man and a woman unite their lives in matrimony. In spite of high divorce rates marriage is still a good thing. In spite of society's controversy over the roles in the family marriage is a fulfillment of both the husband and the wife. God gives us the solution to almost all marital difficulties when He shows us in creation that we are made complete only in our relationship to each other.

FATHER, keep me mindful of what You have given me in my chosen mate. Amen

---

Better is a poor man who walks in his integrity
— Prov. 19:1

Most people I know would like the opportunity to be rich. Get-rich-quick schemes abound and have little trouble attracting clients. But amassing wealth has its own price tag that seekers often overlook in their haste to join that higher economic level. In the beginning the desire for wealth may simply be to better provide for one's family; but like an addictive drug it often becomes an end in itself. This is where noble aims fall by the wayside and honor and integrity are shunted aside as well. It's simply a matter of priorities. We need to continue to keep in focus what is really important to us so that we don't sacrifice that for even admirable, though lesser, goals.

FATHER, remind me to keep my focus on Your will so that the rest of my life will take on proper priorities. Amen

---

He will repay him for his good deed — Prov. 19:17

A certain bubbling joy is available to a person who is willing to do a good deed unnoticed and unrewarded by others. Oh yes, we all like to be appreciated for the work we do. Everyone needs a little pat on the back now and then. But pats on the back, applause, and other similar displays of gratitude soon fade as you and the others go back to your routine. And when we do our good works to be seen and rewarded by others there is always the possibility that no one will take notice. But when we open our heart and our hands to those who cannot repay us or are unaware of what we have done, our joy is made full by the One who sees and is pleased with us.

FATHER, may I be willing to please You today even if no one else ever knows but You and me. Amen

---

What is desirable in a man in his kindness
— Prov. 19:22

What do you look for in the persons you meet for the first time? Some of us look first for beauty of appearance forgetting that such may have no depth. Some look for signs of superior knowledge without concern for whether that is accompanied by wisdom. But whatever a person may lack in all other areas of appearance and personality is easily overshadowed by the one character trait of kindness. With a loving concern for others comes a different kind of beauty of the heart that all the world can see. In kindness toward another a surpassing wisdom shines forth. This one trait makes any person's presence a joy.

FATHER, remind me to be kind from my heart to all I may meet today. Amen

---

Wait for the Lord, and He will save you
— Prov. 20:22

The Scriptures are filled with the promises of God to His children. He assures us continually of His care and His power to help us in our need. But the Bible is also replete with instances in which God's people became so anxious because of their circumstances that they tried to compel God to come in accordance with their own schedule rather than in His good time. In the process we have often gotten ourselves into deeper trouble. Trusting the heavenly Father's love and strength means that we have confidence that He will give us the aid we require at the appropriate time. An old Gospel song is correct in reminding us that "He may not come when we want Him to; but He's always right on time."

FATHER, remind me again that my faith means that I have confidence in You at all times and in all situations. Amen

---

The Lord weighs the hearts — Prov. 21:2

Most of us are quick to judge the rights and wrongs of others. When a good deed is done, especially for us, we seldom stop to ponder the motive that person had for doing what he/she did. We usually want to assume the best in such good doers. However, when another person does something we consider to be wrong we seldom pause to think about the motive for the action. Instead we simply conclude that the person is a bad sort anyway, unless it's someone we think we know well who couldn't possibly have had a bad motive. I am thankful, especially when others do not know my reasons, that my Father knows my heart.

FATHER, help me to know my own heart in what I do today. Amen

---

Victory belongs to the Lord — Prov. 21:31

It is so easy for us to give accolades to the successful businessman or woman. Many companies give bonuses to such stars. Churches that are "successful" give raises to their staffs and sometimes think of them as obviously super saints of God. But for the child of God is whatever field of endeavor there must be a recognition that, at our very best, we are servants of the Most High God. As His servants we do have the privilege of participating in the victory celebration; but the victory is His alone. No matter the level of our achievement, it has been God who worked through us if we accomplished anything worthwhile. For that reason we must always deflect the adulation away from ourselves so that all the glory goes to Him.

FATHER, help me to strive for Your "Well done!" more than any notice others may choose to offer. Amen

------

He who is generous is blessed — Prov. 22:9

Each of us has experienced that good feeling that accompanies giving to someone who is in need. But sometimes we force ourselves into a dilemma trying to determine if the proposed recipient of our generosity is truly deserving. In that process the real joy of giving is lost. That puts us in the position of deciding whether the one in need deserves it more than the one who earned it. Already we are betraying our attachment to our possessions and forgetting that we are only stewards of those things. All the blessings of God are provided so that we may use them to be a blessing to others. And in that giving we find ourselves blessed once more.

FATHER, remind me that all I have is to be used for Your glory, and not just for my benefit. Amen

---

For the Lord will plead their case — Prov. 22:23

Unless you walk through each day with your eyes closed you surely see ample evidence of needs all around you. It is too easy for us, upon seeing the homeless, the abused, the hopeless, to remark that "they ought to do something about that." We know that God cares about such persons and situations and that He will surely do something to alleviate their suffering. What He does is cause us to see it. When believers become aware of these needs it is because the loving Father has opened our eyes and is enlisting our help. The "they" who "ought" becomes us and we must. We are the instruments of His mercy in this world.

FATHER, open my hands as You have opened my eyes so that I may be Your servant today. Amen

---

Do not move the ancient boundary — Prov. 22:28

Within much of society is a desire for continual inno-
vation. We are convinced that what we need in every
case is the new and improved version of everything.
No one wants to hang on to former things for fear of
being thought to be old fashioned. At the same time
there are those who resist all change and improvement just because it is different. Some of these same
sentiments apply in the case of the changing moral
standards that most of us have witnessed during our
lifetime. But there are some boundaries that were
established by the Scriptures. They may come to be
our of fashion but they will never be out of date. They
have been established from eternity and, though they
be old, they are also as up to date as today's sunrise.

FATHER, help me continually search for Your standards
and to be content with them as my guide. Amen

Apply your heart to discipline — Prov. 23:12

The natural tendency of all humans and animals is
to explore the unknown and to try new things. After
all, that is one of the main ways of learning. But
many humans seem to have a bent toward stepping
into those areas others have declared off limits. Even
as children we liked to carefully encroach into those
areas our parents had told us were beyond the boundaries. Something about those things beyond reach has
a strong appeal for many of us. Many of those things

the Scriptures have advised are beyond the line that God has drawn for our good. Like our ancestors in the Garden with everything they needed, we ignore so much of what we are given in pursuit of what we do not need.

FATHER, help me to stay focused on You and Your good gifts so that other things hold no interest for me. Amen

---

Surely there is a future — Prov. 23:18

Ever since mankind devised a way to destroy the planet the inhabitants of our world have had a lingering fear that neither they nor their children would live to a ripe old age. It seems that each day some scientist discovers a part of our normal diet, the air we breathe, or the water we drink that has the potential to kill us. And always lurking nearby are those religious zealots of whatever variety who are preaching doom for all. All the while our heavenly Father reminds His children that, for them at least, all is not lost. In fact for the child of God everything is already gained and we will inherit all of heaven as our eternal home. We flee to the Father, not in fear, but in faith for He is our future.

FATHER, because my present and future are in Your hands I stride forth in confidence to face whatever the world throws at me today. Amen

---

At the last it bites like a serpent — Prov. 23:32

Many experiences, in their beginning, are pleasurable and positive. That one fact often leads us to want to continue the experiences and even add to them. The enjoyment of these activities can be such that they become the very focus of our life. It may well be that only at that point do we begin to see the darker side of these pleasures. Only then does the activity begin to exact its price as it draws us ever deeper into its clutches so that nothing else holds quite the same value any longer. We find ourselves almost helpless to extract ourselves and find that our life with God has suffered more than we knew. But as children of God, the way of repentance always opens the door for our deliverance and return.

FATHER, help me to keep my focus on You so that none of these other things can draw me away. Amen

---

Do not be envious of evil men — Prov. 24:1

Each of us wastes a lot of time. It seems to be connected with the belief that we will have a long life and don't need to worry about it. But believers squander much of their time and energies looking back at their former life or examining the lives of unbelievers to see if they might be enjoying life more than we are. We sometimes behave like a person on a diet looking longingly at some luscious dessert that has a million calories. But as believers we are not merely on a diet that has eliminated the fun things of the evil world. As followers after God we have a new life in which those desires are no longer part of our character. That which brings joy to us now is related to pleasing our Savior and lifting up others in His name.

FATHER, remind me again today of the greater joys that I have found in You. Amen

———————

Do not rejoice when your enemy falls — Prov. 24:17

Believers have always had difficulty in dealing with their enemies. From the earliest days of the Christian era when some wanted to call fire down from heaven on their perceived enemies to modern day bashing of those with whom we have differing political views. We really do have difficulty loving those who have differing opinions. Sometimes we even tell ourselves that we "have to love them because God told us to, but we don't have to like them." Love is never a "have to" thing. Love is a choice, a commitment we make because of Him who has loved us. We also forget that God loves and blesses whom He chooses, not just those who happen to be on our side.

FATHER, deliver me from my assumptions of rightness so that I may declare Your rightness in all things. Amen

———————

Do not fret because of evil-doers — Prov. 24:19

Oftentimes because we happen to be in a minority on some issue we find it easy to just throw up our hands and do nothing. We think that our contribution to an issue is worthless since the majority are going in what we believe to be the wrong direction. We must remember that the forces of evil in the world will always be more numerous than the righteous. However, our Father has always specially blessed His "remnant" not for being victorious in the battles of this world but for being faithful to Him. And, even better, we know a secret about the future that the workers of wickedness do not know. We know that our Father will be victorious when it really counts – at the end.

FATHER, thank You for encouraging me to remain faithful though many others may not. Amen

———————————

The Lord will reward you — Prov. 25:22

Most of the people in the world labor in the shadows while a few get the attention and, often, the material rewards. Those not in the limelight continue on with their tasks, usually without complaint, knowing that their work is important to them and their families and even to the overall function of the group for which they work. But we do get discouraged sometimes because the twilight where we labor makes it increasingly difficult to provide for those we love.

Nevertheless, we will continue faithful because we are believers and would not wish to dishonor our Father y less than our best. After all, we are confident that He sees our work and recognizes our devotion to Him and will present to us His own reward.

FATHER, I commit my energies to glorifying You today in all that I do. Amen

---

Nor is it glory to search out one's own glory
— Prov. 25:27

Do you understand why you do a good, or bad, job at your place of employment or in your tasks in your home? You may do less than your best because you feel that you are not appreciated. You may work very hard because your supervisor or family members continually encourage you. But you may also do your work the way you do so that you will be noticed and given recognition. However, if you are working primarily for the praise of others that adulation will leave you somewhat empty. Seeking recognition and praise leads us in an increasingly demanding struggle that we will eventually lose. God's favor, on the other hand, can never be achieved. It can only be given because of His unconditional love.

FATHER, I yearn for the glow of Your smile that comes only because You love me. Amen

---

Do you see a man wise in his own eyes?
— *Prov. 26:12*

Ego is a very important part of the makeup of every individual. It is that part of us that gives us a vision of who and what we are. When it is functioning properly that vision approximates reality. However, there are many of us, including many believers who place little value on themselves. Such low self-esteem is sometimes mistaken for humility. But God places great value on each one of us because we are His children and He loves us with abandon. There are others who see themselves as more than they actually are. This kind of pride fosters feelings of superiority. There may be nothing quite so deflating to the ego as finding out you are not as smart or as strong as you thought you were. Thankfully, God's Spirit helps give balance to our self-image.

FATHER, keep me mindful of who I am in relation to You. Amen

————————————

For lack of wood the fire goes out (and where there is no whisperer) — *Prov. 26:20*

Words have such tremendous power to heal and to injure. In our culture they seem most often to be used to bring down rather than build up. Sometimes the injury is only loosely based on facts and mostly on speculation and innuendo. Though "sticks and stones" may still break bones, words can break spirit and demean character and reputation. Though we may not be guilty of starting rumors, we are often carriers. We fail to appreciate the fact that repeating rumors also adds fuel to them. We don't have to argue against the rumors. Refusing to pass them on to others has the same effect as a firebreak to a raging forest fire.

FATHER, help me to refrain my tongue from being an instrument for spreading injury. Amen

———————————

Let another praise you — Prov. 27:1

We are so proud or our accomplishments, even if our own wisdom, planning, and skill had little to do with them. We want the whole world to know the good things about us. When they are slow to take notice we may even want to draw their attention to those things we have done. But what we must avoid is getting the "pride shoulder" which is a pain in that joint caused by trying to pat ourselves on the back. It is much sweeter to bask in the glow of praise when it comes from the lips of someone else who has recently discovered your real worth. It is most glorious when that praise comes from the Father who sees even those things you have done in secret.

FATHER, help me to live today in the knowledge that it is only Your praise that really matters. Amen

———————————

*He who cares for his master will be honored
— Prov. 27:18*

There is no place for half-heartedness in a believer. It is too often the case with some believers that they develop such a "this world is not my home" mentality that they give little concern to the activities and duties of their earthly life. We may even get so busy serving the Lord that we let other things slide. But we must remember that God is not honored if we neglect any of our duties, even those to our employer. If we serve our employer well we will be honored by God even if not honored by the employer. And, of course, when we serve our heavenly Father well He will give us the greatest honor by being pleased with us.

FATHER, help me to work well so that You are honored in all of my life. Amen

---

Riches are not forever — Prov. 27:24

Every one of us would like to have the assurance that our latter years will be financially comfortable. For that reason most of us are willing to spend the time and the money planning and providing for those years. Sadly in the process we may begin to lose our focus and become enamored simply with the idea of making more money. Also in that process we lose sight of other important things like family and church. When we die is it more important to leave our family financially comfortable or to leave them with the memory of our love and of meaningful time spent with them? Only one of those things is guaranteed to stay with them no matter what.

FATHER, help me to keep the material things in my life as servants, not allowing them to gain mastery of me. Amen

---

Even his prayer is an abomination — Prov 28:9

Among those who profess the Christian faith there is often a variation between profession and action. In those times in history when religion of any kind had a favorable reputation there were always pretenders to the faith who wanted to associate with good people though not becoming one of them. For those folks it is all a sham. They may participate in all the activities of the faithful without the heart-changing commitment to being one of the faithful. All of their "religiosity" is a mockery of real faith and is anathema. And there is a little of this hypocrisy in most of us. We need to constantly submit our lives to the Father for examination and cleansing.

FATHER, cleanse me today from that falseness that would lead others astray. Amen

---

A faithful man will abound with blessings
— Prov. 28:20

All of us have known persons who were apparently faithful to God, sometimes to a degree that makes us ashamed of our own commitment to Him. We have also seen many of them experience such dire circumstances that would cause the rest of us to crumble. Yet they have remained strong. And through it all their faith has seemed, if anything, to get even stronger. A casual look at their lives would seem to contradict this assertion of Scripture. But just talk to them and you will learn of blessings you never saw. You will hear from them of blessings without number that overshadow any difficulties they may have known.

FATHER, in all my circumstances help me to look for Your loving hand at work to bless me. Amen

---

The righteous sings and rejoices — Prov. 29:6

Many of the religions of the world are characterized by somberness and quiet reflection. Though there is a place for some of this in the life of Christian believers, this is not to be the primary trait. Among believers there is even a time for sorrow; but that is not the overriding frame of mind for the child of God. How can a person who has literally been snatched from the jaws of certain eternal death not burst forth with joy? When we contemplate the awesome nature of the God who stepped into human history to be a sacrifice for our sin, how can we restrain a joyful song? We have received the most glorious news that God loves us without restraint and we cannot keep silent.

FATHER, as I think of You today I know I must sing in my heart regardless of my circumstances. Amen

———————

A wise man holds back [his temper] — Prov. 29:11

Very little good is ever accomplished by outbursts of anger. Usually when we blow up over some incident we decide later that we over-reacted or were just plain wrong. When we unleash our wrath it never seems to make us feel better as we had hoped. And sometimes the full brunt of our temper ends up hurting someone, often the wrong one. Our anger is often simply a way of seeking revenge for some wrong someone appears to have done us. But vengeance is never truly sweet as is advertised. Controlling our anger helps to give us control over the situation. God will repay those who have really wronged us. And furthermore, His judgment is intended to restore and not just to hurt.

FATHER, I willingly leave to You any punishment necessary for those who wrong me. Amen

———————

> *Where there is no vision, the people are*
> *unrestrained — Prov. 29:18*

When we contemplate the world around us with all its wickedness and fearfulness, we would be miserable creatures if we thought that life would always be that way or worse. Living in this world with no hope for tomorrow and beyond could, and does, lead many to conclude that their way of life does not matter. As a result they might easily determine to go for all the pleasure immediate life offers them. But when we know we will be held accountable we quickly become more restrained in our behavior. And when we understand that Hod has a purpose for each of His creatures we begin to see our life in the context of His loving plan and we reach forward to each new day with a hope that lifts us from our current circumstances.

FATHER, I glory in the hope You have set before me that draws me ever hearer to You. Amen

---

Justice for man comes from the Lord — Prov. 29:26

Many persons in these days are looking for justice. We want those who have wronged us to be punished. We even want those whom we believe to have wronged someone else to get what they've got coming to them. We seem to always be looking for punishment for all those who have broken the rules except ourselves. For ourselves we want mercy and understanding.

But we need to remember that justice, when it comes from the Father, is always good for us. His justice does not have punishment for its goal. Rather, God's justice is designed to effect redemption and restoration. With that in mind we may seek His justice for ourselves and others with joy.

FATHER, because I know I can trust You, I joyfully commit Myself to Your will for me. Amen

------

"I have done no wrong" — *Prov. 30:20*

Not one of us would say that, because we have been taught in Church all our lives that none of us is "sin-free." Yet we are not really bad people, are we? We can scroll down through the Ten Commandments and come up with pretty high marks. We may have committed some of the little wrongs, but none of the real biggies like murder. For that reason we easily make a distinction between ourselves and those "worthless" creatures who live in certain areas of town or wind up behind bars. But we have all come short of God's desire for us and are in need of His redemption. The only one who has "done no wrong" has taken upon Himself our sins so that we may be made clean through Him.

FATHER, I give You thanks that You wash me and make me clean in spite of myself and my sin. Amen

------

*The churning of anger produces strife
— Prov. 30:33*

Why would anyone deliberately make someone else angry? Perhaps the idea is to taunt someone who is smaller or weaker just for sport. Perhaps the notion is to see how far one can go with a stronger person before making him angry. Whatever the plan might be, there is always danger in stirring the wrath of another person. When anger wells up inside one easily loses rationality and acts from emotion rather than good sense. When anger spills over, all who are within reach are at risk, even the person who is angry. Those who deliberately rouse the anger of someone else should be aware that they may get caught in its fire as well.

FATHER, teach me to incite to love that produces peace rather than anger which seldom profits. Amen

---

*Open your mouth ... for the rights of all the
unfortunate — Prov.31:8)*

Sometimes believers who become involved in meeting the material needs of people are scorned, even by other believers, as "do-gooders." Now isn't that a terrible name! To be accused of trying to help persons in need puts you in a category all of us should be proud to be in. Those of us who have been so blessed by the Father have a holy obligation to share with those who have less. That is one means at hand by which we can show the love of Christ. Our Father needs us to not only do what we can in a material way but to lift our voices as advocates for those who have no real voice.

FATHER, remind me to use the influence I have to speak out for those who have no other voice but mine. Amen

---

She does him good and not evil — Prov. 31:12

Often we get the notion that we can be neutral toward someone. But how is that possible? In the effort to be neutral you would be required to IGNORE the other person. To ignore another person created in the image of God would mean that we would behave as though they did not exist. Throughout history this was the way one treated a slave – as though they were non-persons. Is that not itself evil? Recognizing that everyone is a creation of God and loved by Him can help give us the proper perspective. Even by denying our love we are doing evil to others. Those whom we love and respect are those we want to do good for.

FATHER, lead me to active goodness toward those I encounter this day. Amen

---

A woman who fears the Lord ... shall be praised
— Prov. 31:30

Our society has traditionally put a lot of stress on appearance and on achievement in the roles given to the sexes. In spite of the changing attitudes toward women and their role in society and in the church, many of us still put our major emphasis on their fulfilling the traditional image. In the same manner men are not men if they do not care for the traditionally "male" activities. Women with a career in the public sector and men who choose a career in the arts are similarly suspect in their gender roles. However, the Scriptures remind us that the most important role for a woman or a man is that of believer. Only from that beginning point can either find fulfillment in life.

FATHER, create in me more concern for comforming to Your image that any image society may expect of me. Amen

ECCLESIASTES

Listening to the Preacher

Man is not able to tell it — Eccl. 1:8

Throughout history mankind has responded to the unknown in two basic ways. We have either accepted it as unknowable and therefore feared it or ignored it, or we have accepted it as a challenge and something of an affront to our intellect and bent all our energies to uncovering its mysteries. But even as our information about things expands it seems that the things we still want to know increases. The mysteries of God are especially that way. The more we come to know God and know about Him the more we are continually humbled by the vastness of what we don't understand. It is when we think we know Him best that we have closed our hearts to knowing Him more.

FATHER, open my eyes that I may see more of You and my mind that I may hunger to know more of You. Amen

In much wisdom there is much grief — Eccl. 1:18

A popular old prayer encourages us to gain serenity in the face of the knowledge that there are some situations we cannot change. However, the more we really understand matters in this life the more we become frustrated at our lack of ability to open the eyes of others to these things. Surely one of the great roles of wisdom in any life is to seek the increase of wisdom in the lives of many others. The grief of wisdom would then be seeing the willingness of so many to reject wisdom for the bliss of ignorance. The truly wise must surely be continually brought to sorrow over this folly and more determined to bring them to the light of understanding.

FATHER, may whatever wisdom You have given me drive me to help others come to know Your truth. Amen

---

"Come now, I will test you with pleasure"
— Eccl. 2:1

Surely everyone wants to feel good. And we must remember that finding pleasure in various activities of life is not even discouraged in the Scriptures. However, you have probably noticed that most of us spend an inordinate amount of our lives seeking those things that will give us pleasure. Even some of the otherwise good things we do are somewhat sullied by our doing them primarily for the good feeling we will derive from the deed. The desire for that good feeling quickly distracts us from our worthy goal and becomes the substitute. When that occurs we are soon drawn into a kind of slavery to that pleasure which had been such a wonderful by-product of a much higher aim.

FATHER, thank You for the pleasure derived from serving You while serving is still the goal. Amen

---

All that my eyes desired I did not refuse them
— Eccl. 2:10

Many of us may fantasize about being freed from all the restrictions that seem to abound in the life of ordinary persons, especially those who are believers. But, rather than imagine what pleasures that kind of life might afford, all we need to do is look around us. You know of that section of your city where it seems that nearly all the restrictions of decent behavior have been abandoned. You may have even seen some of the people who frequent those areas at a time when they had finished gorging themselves on all sorts of self-destructive behavior. When you have seen this you begin to revise the list of things you might desire and are grateful that your conscience and the Spirit dwelling in you lead you in the better way.

FATHER, quench in me the desire to step across Your lines so that my heart's desire may be filled by You alone. Amen

---

The wise man and the fool alike die! — Eccl. 2:16

The biblical writers long ago reminded mankind that death is an appointment all of us must keep. In spite of all the advancements in science and technology no one has discovered the miracle diet or the fool-proof exercise plan that will permanently stave off the summons of death. The fool may determine to live as though death will never come except to others; but that often leads to its arrival even more quickly. The prudent man, too, will die; but death will not come as a fearful intruder to snatch us away from life. Instead, the truly wise person has prepared for that time by trusting in the grace of God through Jesus Christ. Death, then, is merely the gateway to the fuller dimensions of life everlasting with the Father.

FATHER, keep me from becoming so obsessed with death, or even the life hereafter, that I forget to live for You now. Amen

---

I must leave it to the man who will come after me
— Eccl. 2:18

Few of us need to be reminded that our life on this earth is only temporary. We are faced with the evidence daily that human life is fragile at best. And yet, so many of us plan earthly life as though it will last forever because we make so little preparation for life after that. We "lay up for ourselves treasures on earth" with great care even though we are aware that we must one day leave it all behind. Even though believers know that one day they will leave this earth for their final home in heaven, most of us have only made the preparation of getting our ticket. We would serve ourselves well to spend much more of our energies on those things which are eternal.

FATHER, help me to focus more of my attention on those things that will not die with me or be left behind me. Amen

———————

Who can have enjoyment without Him?
— Eccl. 2:25

Our world is fascinated with having fun. We are willing to spend a large portion of our income to have fun. We even look around us to see if there is anyone having more fun than us and, if so, we envy them and try our best to match their level of enjoyment. But those who are addicted to such pleasures are never satisfied for long. They must continually increase their level of excitement and pleasure to get that same feeling. In the end they are always left empty. But the believer has discovered that the real source of all joy is in the saving relationship with Jesus Christ. Apart from Him there can be no lasting enjoyment.

FATHER, I thank You for Your joy which has flooded over me since I came to know You as Savior. Amen

---

There is an appointed time for everything
— Eccl. 3:1

Much of the time when believers look at this passage they recall many of the sermons they have heard exhorting them to prepare for the time of their death. That is definitely a crucial event for which everyone must be prepared. However, there are many other "appointed" times in the believer's life. Because these are appointed by God they are also of utmost importance. Any time we hear the voice of God calling us we are facing one of these times scheduled by Him. These opportunities for obedience and service will not come again. They may not be postponed to a more convenient time for us. If we miss these appointments we miss out on special blessings from God and are forever poorer for it.

FATHER, help me to listen for You today with hands and feet and tongue ready to do Your bidding without hesitation. Amen

---

He has also set eternity in their heart — Eccl. 3:11

Humankind has always wondered and speculated about tomorrow. Though some seem only to live for today, we all have dreams and hopes related to the future. For many these images are faint and destined to fade into disappointment. But even in the face of disappointment hopes are reborn slightly refashioned to give us the gumption to face life again. Our spirit will just not allow us to believe that our current circumstances are the final answer to life. "There must be something more!" is what the heart cries in its depths and even in the exhilaration of its mountaintops. That yearning is for a greater existence than this. That hunger is for the life that only God can give and that gift He offers us through His Son.

FATHER, help me to live today in the assurance that my life with You has only just begun. Amen

_____

There is nothing better ... than to rejoice
and do good — Eccl.3:12)

Each of us has different priorities in life. Earning a living for ourselves and our family is always high on the list, as it should be. But most of us have daily schedules that are so full that some very important aspects of life get squeezed out simply for lack of time. Whatever spare time we have may reasonably be spent on our own enjoyment. The tragedy often is that we limit our enjoyment to those things that are done directly for ourselves. We easily overlook the thrill received as a by-product of something done for others. You remember how it felt the last time you did something like that. Doesn't that make you want to do it again, and often?

Father, help me never to grow tired of doing good. Amen

Everything God does will remain forever
— Eccl. 3:14

The work of God is never done in half measure. With the Creator there are no temporary "stop gap" solutions. All of His work is part of His glorious and holy idea begun in the creation. All of His efforts to recall mankind from the edge of that chasm which drops away into eternal darkness have been only part of His gracious plan that culminated in the work of Christ from Bethlehem through the open door of the garden tomb. His work of redemption in each of our lives is no less eternal. Scripture assures us that the work He has begun in us will not be cut short by any lurings of the evil one. Instead, it is God's honor on the line for He has promised to bring His work in us to completion. God be praised!

Father, I submit myself to Your continuing work in me today to bring me to that glorious completion You have promised. Amen

---

God will judge both the righteous man and the
wicked man — Eccl. 3:17

Everyone who knows anything about God knows that the wicked person is definitely going to be judged by

Him and face eternal condemnation. Believers have heard their preachers lambaste sinners in the pews with threats of fire and brimstone as their just punishment. We know that to escape that fate we must turn to the Lord. But far too many of us forget that God's judgment is not limited to the wicked. Every one of us will give account of himself to God. The sins of the believer are not overlooked. God will surely punish us for our sins, but He will not banish us from His presence. Though we will suffer for our wrongdoing, Jesus paid the ultimate penalty for those who trust Him. Hallelujah!

FATHER, though Your chastening causes me pain, I am thankful of the assurance of continuing to be part of Your family. Amen

———————

They had no one to comfort them — Eccl. 4:1

While most of us live with relative plenty, we cannot ignore the fact that countless millions in our world are poor and diseased with little hope that their life will ever be improved. We witness their pitiful forms on television as some advocates try to shame us into parting with some of our abundance that their lives might know some small blessing. In the days of long ago God saw that the whole world was without hope. Both rich and poor were existing and yet neither had any real future. In His great mercy toward us He revealed His presence to the world in Jesus born in

Bethlehem. His long awaited birth brought encouragement and hope to the whole race of humanity.

FATHER, use me today to bring Your encouragement to those I will meet. Amen

———————

One will lift up his companion — Eccl. 4:10

Around the holidays we are reminded in the midst of our own joy of family and friends that many do not have that same experience. On many days throughout the year there are those whose lives are lonely or even shattered by some devastating loss. We may feel sorry for them though we seldom let that sadness dampen our own good time. But what they need is not our pity but our companionship. They need US! On each good day we have it is important for us to seek out those who are having less than a good day. We may easily be the one bright spark of light in their life that day which gives them the courage to continue living.

FATHER, remind me to share the joy I have in You with someone else today. Amen

———————

Who no longer knows how to receive instruction
— Eccl. 4:13

Watching children grow is exciting. I often envy teachers who get to be present when their students, our children, make some of the great discoveries of life. What joy it must be to observe young minds open and anxious to absorb knowledge that will prepare them to face life. The sad thing is to see those who have decided that they have nothing to learn from others any longer. Perhaps this happens to those who are duped by their own desire for independence and have thereby condemned themselves to their own devices. Others have, just as sadly, decided that they are no longer capable of learning and have thereby condemned themselves to huddling in cold isolation while the world passes them by. All living things must grow or die.

FATHER, I open my heart today to learn more of You. Amen

Guard your steps as you go to the house of God
— Eccl. 5:1

It is almost common among church-goers that they put their best foot forward when they go to church. For many, church behavior is vastly different from Monday through Saturday life. Entering the church means a different vocabulary, different friends, different attire, and even a different facial expression for some. Sadly our preparations for the church event don't begin until Saturday night or Sunday morning. No wonder the activities of that day are such a whirl-wind that they leave us exhausted. What if every day were lived in preparation for the Lord's Day? Drastic changes would be unnecessary and the whole week would build toward Sunday which would then erupt into glad praise and worship of the heavenly Father.

FATHER, build in me each day a longing to worship You along with my brothers and sisters in the faith. Amen

———————————

Do not let your speech cause you to sin — Eccl. 5:6

You learn a lot about a person's character by listening to what they talk about when they are with friends or work associates. Sadly, except perhaps for the vocabulary, the conversation among believers and that among non-believers is very similar. It is not simply that we talk about others but that we talk about them in a destructive manner. We might excuse ourselves by saying that our comments are true. But whatever we say to others or about others must always be designed to uplift and not to tear down. We are easily seduced into making derogatory comments even about our friends. It is difficult to guard our tongue so that we do not drag ourselves down in the midst of dragging down others.

FATHER, make my words soothing to the spirit and calming to the soul of those I speak with today. Amen

———————————

He who loves money will not be satisfied
— Eccl. 5:10

We've all heard the comment about some people that "they'll do anything for a dollar." Thankfully most of us are not like that. We convince ourselves that we are not like that at all. But what we talk about and think about a lot surely has a high priority in our lives. For many of us one of those topics is money. Some of us are consumed by scheming for more or worrying about having too little. The more we think about it the more it occupies our thoughts, crowding out the really important matters. For the believer, where is the loving admonition of Jesus not to fret (think too much) about such things? Doesn't our Father care more about us than the flowers of the field and the birds of the air?

FATHER, fill my thoughts with Yourself so that all the other matters of life may take their proper place. Amen

---

The sleep of the working man is pleasant
— Eccl. 5:12

For some folks the idea of success is to get rich enough that they don't have to work. On the surface that may sound attractive. But none of us was designed for sustained leisure. We all like to have some leisure time but we soon get bored and need something productive to do. Many of us have discovered that it is when we are idle that we begin to fret or to devise some activity that is not good for us or others. When we have been involved in some labor that has earned our wages or has benefited someone else we are able to feel a sense of accomplishment that pushes aside some of the concerns that would otherwise flood our minds and steal away our time of refreshment and rest.

FATHER, keep me engaged in the business of life so that I may refresh myself with the thought of having contributed to the lives of others. Amen

---

God keeps him occupied with the gladness of his heart — Eccl. 5:20

Have you seen them at your workplace or even in your neighborhood? They aren't difficult to recognize because they are so different from the norm. In fact it is for that reason that many of them are considered to be mentally disturbed or at least out of touch with reality. They seem to move through daily life with a peace that belies circumstances much like our own that almost cripple us. They are not insulated from the often sharp edges of life but they seem able to absorb the painful aspects of life without being mortally wounded by them. It's as though they are being carried along with some holy "adrenaline" that pushes them past the pains because of the joy set before them.

FATHER, fill me with Yourself so that Your presence in me will touch the lives of those around me. Amen

---

But his soul is not satisfied with good things
— Eccl. 6:3

Contentment just seems not to be built into humanity. Our dissatisfaction with the status quo can be that which drives us to change things for the better. It is just that sort of discontent with the way things were that drove our forefathers to search for freedom. But it is also an angry form of that which has caused the great struggles for power that have overthrown governments. Some aims in life are so shallow and unworthy that when they have been achieved leave a dryness in the soul that longs for still more. Few of those who have achieved positions of power or great wealth are ever satisfied without still more. Contentment is only to be found in being right with God. Only in that blessed relationship can we find the One who satisfies in spite of circumstances.

FATHER, help me to be content in You in spite of my circumstances. Amen

---

Who can tell a man what will be after him
— Eccl. 6:12

One of the characteristics of humanity that separates us from the rest of the animal world is that our hearts can see beyond what our eyes can behold. Only those who have had humanity taken from them by continual oppressive circumstances live in dread of what another day will bring and dare not lift their eyes to the distant horizon. We seem to have a hunger for what is still beyond us and that keeps us reaching out to the future. But what will that time hold for us? None of us knows with certainty. But we can know the One for whom the future is just as clear as the present and the past. He is the guardian and the preparer of life here and the life in our eternity with Him.

FATHER, I trust You with all my tomorrows. Amen

It is better to listen to the rebuke of a wise man
— Eccl. 7:5

Criticism is not something that anyone really looks forward to unless they have some masochistic bent. Most of us would prefer to hear good things about ourselves even if we suspect that the praise is slightly less than accurate. Throughout history persons of power were able to surround themselves with these purveyors of "white lies." We all want words of encouragement. But what value is a praise for speed to a person you know is headed in the wrong direction? Sometimes the best kind of encouragement is a word of correction or even rebuke when we are not conducting ourselves in the way we ought. A parent or other friend who only praises us may be guilty of abetting behavior that will one day destroy us.

FATHER, thank you for Your correction even in those times when I may resent it for the moment. Amen

---

Do not be eager in your heart to be angry
— Eccl. 7:9

Some people seem to go through life with a chip on their shoulder just daring anyone to cross them so that they can explode. They seem to be absorbed in the effort to find fault. Anyone who ventures to speak to someone operating in this mode is liable to be attacked. One may wonder if such a person just got up on the wrong side of the bed or if the problem goes deeper. The believer has no reason to be angry at the world. Neither does a believer have reason to live life on the edge of a grudge against everyone or anyone. Our Lord taught us not to keep records of the sins of others against us but to seek, rather, to forgive. We must remember the example of our heavenly Father who has spent all of history providing for forgiveness rather than wrath.

FATHER, teach me to love in ways that evoke a spirit of forgiveness instead of anger. Amen

---

Do not be excessively righteous — Eccl. 7:15

What a startling admonition to find in Scripture! In all of your life you have probably known no one who really fit in this category. Being too good has never been a problem. However, in a day when so many seem to be driven to overachieve, it may be that this is a warning against trying to earn greater favor from God because of our super-human efforts to be good. More likely the concern of God's Word is that insidious craving to appear to be much better than we really are. Many in Jesus' day prided themselves on living by the Law better than the masses. Yet it was those persons who were often the object of Jesus' wrath for simply putting on a show of goodness while inside being children of hell.

FATHER, remind me that I can never meet your standard of goodness in my own strength. Amen

---

God made men upright, but they have sought ...
— Eccl. 7:29

Most of us understand that when God created the world it was as He intended and was also heading in the direction He had designed. The Bible tells us that this was true of mankind as well. All seemed to be in harmony throughout the universe. The Tempter was present but had not yet brought them into sin. We do not know how many times the Tempter had tried to lure them away before he succeeded. We do know that once they sought something outside His good purpose for them the harmony with God was broken. The story has continued the same throughout all our generations. Seeking after something on the fringes of danger has been our way and we have paid dearly for our search.

FATHER, teach me to seek more Your will than my own. Amen

―――――――――

Wisdom ... causes his stern face to beam
― Eccl. 8:1

To walk among the poor, the homeless, the hope-less, is usually a journey into a land of bitterness and depression. Those whose lives are characterized by such have come to understand that their future will be no different from their current circumstances. They feel condemned because they know nothing else in life. Material help for those persons is never the final answer. To some degree each one of us has been there. Before we found the peace that comes only through faith we too were poor and hopeless. With that peace has come a new outlook on life and an understanding of our place in things. With that comes a joy that wells up within us to overflow to all those around us.

FATHER, thank You for Your grace and peace which cause my little light to shine in spite of any circum-stance. Amen

―――――――――

Evil will not deliver those who practice it
— Eccl. 8:8

When you do something you should not have done you normally go through a fairly standard procedure. First, you may look around to see if anyone else caught you in the act. Then you might move on to try to figure out if there is anyway you can rationalize or justify your behavior. If none of these ploys works you might decide to lie about it or blame someone else for the problem. But even if any of these efforts is successful with relation to those to whom you are responsible, there is still One who sees all and from whom we have no place to hide. Before Him there is no alternative but to repent so that real healing can take place and life can get back on track.

FATHER, I lay myself before Your mercy seat in the name of Jesus. Amen

---

It will be well for those who fear the Lord
— Eccl. 8:12

We must never presume that just because we are believers we will never have problems or go through hard times. In fact we can count on those things being part of life. Our Lord prepared us for such when He was in flesh among us. He showed us in His life and teaching that in some ways we might have even more troubles because of our faith. But God's Word also plainly teaches the believer that whatever difficulties thrown at us by Satan or by circumstances our Father is always at work to bring about a blessing for us through those things. Though we may have a hard time seeing these blessings because of the present hardship, we can still be confident that God is already actively turning our tears into joy and gladness.

FATHER, in the midst of my trouble remind me of the triumph that is already mine because of Your great love for me. Amen

---

Their deeds are in the hand of God — Eccl. 9:1

Each of us appreciates having our good deeds acknowledged by others. Though we may declare otherwise we probably would all like a pat on the back or a round of applause when we have done a good job or given of ourselves by "going the second mile." But sometimes those acts of kindness and generosity must be done in a way so that others never find out about it. When we have done those things we have discovered a special joy in that anonymity. It is made even more special when, as a believer, we know that even the things we have done in secret are known to our heavenly Father. That knowledge gives us strength and encouragement to continue in that work.

FATHER, thank You for the opportunity to serve You by doing good for others. Amen

---

Man does not know his time — Eccl. 9:12

Envisioning and planning for the future are abilities open only to humans on this planet. Some of us do it better than others but each of us may do so. When we look toward the future we hope that all will go well then plan for the possibility that the opposite will come to pass. Many of the events we plan for are normal for people like us. In recent years a lot of emphasis has even begun to be placed on preparing for death. We know that each one of us will die, however, none of us knows precisely when that time will come. The Bible continually exhorts us to be prepared for that eventuality whenever it may occur. The most important preparation we may make is to trust ourselves to God for His salvation.

FATHER, remind me that trusting You is not a one time event but a lifelong commitment to You. Amen

---

One sinner destroys much good — Eccl. 9:17

All of us have known of manufactured items that contained an imperceptible flaw which, in time, caused the item to become dangerous or worthless. We have seen great enterprises brought down by the misconduct of some key personnel. Some of us have known of great churches being brought down by one person spreading lies and rumors about the leaders of the congregation. We don't always need to look very far to find the culprit. You or I may even be guilty of being that "bad apple that spoiled the whole barrel" of some worthy enterprise. Satan gladly assists any one of us who through jealousy or greed want to damage some work that God is doing through others.

FATHER, because of Your love for me do not allow me to be an instrument of Satan today. Amen

---

Folly is set in many exalted places — Eccl. 10:6

In former times in the history of humanity those who were leaders were those who could demonstrate that they were wiser than their colleagues. Gradually this practice was set aside when strong men learned that they could take control and hire a wise man to give them direction. As power increased the willingness to listen to wise men decreased. Instead, the strong leader gathered around himself those who would tell him what he wanted to hear. Now in a day when most of the world chooses its own leaders we have begun to put persons in those positions who tell us what we want to hear. We are willing to accept the folly of our leaders because we are blinded by our own. The folly is now so widespread we are hardly able to recognize wise persons among us and usually consign them to the shadows.

FATHER, help me not to fall victim to the folly of others by first recognizing in my own life. Amen

---

He who digs a pit may fall into it — Eccl. 10:8

Few, if any, of us can endure a person who is always working to undermine the work and reputation of another. Many of you have been the victim of some malicious plan. In our better moments we find it difficult to believe that a person would deliberately scheme to harm someone else. Yet, in a worse moment we may have considered such a plot ourselves because someone has hurt us in some way. When we engage in such planning we need to remember that almost every such scheme ends up injuring the planner as much or more than the intended victim. On the other hand, when we strive to do good to those who hurt us we end up receiving a blessing for ourselves.

FATHER, teach me to be a blessing even to those who plot evil against me. Amen

---

If a man should live many years, let him rejoice in them all — Eccl. 11:8

The human race, at least in modern times, is a bunch of "wishers." No matter our current situation, we find something lacking and wish we were in some other situation. We can be happy for a brief time but are never satisfied for long. When we are very young we wish to be older. In our middle years we can't wait to retire. As the aches and pains of older age become constant companions we yearn for those former carefree days of youth. But each day of our life on this earth is a day God crafted specially for His children. It is a time to spend in fruitful labor, a time to spend with family and friends, and a time to spend in reflection and communion with the heavenly Father. With those things in mind any day of any year can be a good one.

FATHER, help me to see the good things in this day so that I may be a blessing to someone else. Amen

---

Childhood and the prime of life are fleeting
— Eccl. 11:10

Anyone who is unaware of the speed with which youth disappears is obviously still in the middle of it. When we are young we find it difficult to imagine ever getting old like some of those we see from time to time. Even when we thought about growing old we always envisioned it somewhere off in the distant future. Then one day we looked around and realized that the distant future was at hand. That is when we begin to imagine how our life could have been different. Many things come to mind that we wish we had done or not done. Regrets are multiplied as we recall missed opportunities of younger days. Unlike the games we played as kids, life has no "do-overs." However our Father does allow us a new beginning in Christ, which makes it possible to be forgiven and get new direction for the future.

FATHER, thank You for delivering me from living in regret by giving me a new future in Christ. Amen

---

Remember ... your Creator in the days of your youth
— Eccl. 12:1

The Preacher has throughout this short book spoken of his search for the meaning of life. Having apparently been surrounded with the trappings of wealth and power all his days he has found himself strangely empty. None of the things he has been able to provide for himself has brought the satisfaction he had hoped. Then, perhaps near the end of his days, he looks back over what might have been had he not become distracted with having. Many of us have a similar story. Many more of us will before our life is done. What a tragedy to allow ourselves to be lured away from the only One who brings purpose to life!

FATHER, I beg Your forgiveness for time wasted on matters that have such little eternal value. Amen

---

The words of wise men are like goads
— (Eccl. 12:11)

All of us place high value on words of wisdom in times of uncertainty and lack of direction. When we want help we seek out those who have the kind of knowledge we think will be beneficial in our situa-

232

tion. However, when our minds are set on a particular course we reject guidance from anyone not interested in going along with us. Words of wisdom are not so welcome when we are determined to do something foolish. We don't even want to hear such words because they expose our foolishness and make us uncomfortable with our chosen path. On the other hand, when we have strayed into that path, the words of the wise prod us back toward the paths where we know we belong.

FATHER, thank You for the goads You send to me in love so that I may stay on Your path for me. Amen

---

God will bring every act to judgment — Eccl. 12:4

There are no secrets with God. We may well appear to be blameless before our neighbors and co-workers while carrying on rank immorality behind closed doors. But probably our own case is not that extreme. We are neither blameless nor do we live a life of total depravity. We live more in that "gray" area between the two. We may even excuse ourselves by saying that we are no worse than others; but that really doesn't excuse us or them. The fact remains that appearances don't carry much weight with God when we are trying to hide our sins. He holds us responsible, not just for what others can see in us, but what He sees in our hearts. There are no secrets with God.

FATHER, cleanse me of the sin that so easily besets me so that I can live real life in Your presence. Amen

---

SONG
of
SOLOMON

Meditating on Love

The king has brought me into his chambers
— Song of Sol. 1:4

This marvelous little book of love poems between a groom and his bride have been fittingly applied by Christians to the intimate love relationship between Christ and His church. Such intimacy is seen clearly in this opening passage by the invitation into private communion with Him. This is the place where our spirit communes with Him in ways beyond words and our experience of His nearness brings us a joy that bids us yield ourselves to Him with nothing of ourselves held back. Why would we deny anything of ourselves to the One who has already demonstrated His love by giving His all to us and for us? He woos us with His love to come to Him.

FATHER, Your invitation to intimacy with You is at once exhilarating and disturbing because You give so much and I can bring so little. Amen

---

He has brought me to his banquet hall
— Song of Sol. 2:4

We have never been very good children of God individually. Neither have we ever been a faithful and pure bride as a church. We might easily wonder why the Father has not put this Bride aside and started over. And yet Jesus, in His love that was willing to die for us, loves us with an everlasting love. The Father, in His mercy that cared for us even in our sin, will not let us go. And more than that, He proudly owns us as His children. Though we have shamed Him in countless ways in our sin and rebellion, He is still proud to have us. Though we have withheld ourselves and our meager goods from Him, He brings us into His bounty as His honored guests even as part of His royal family.

FATHER, Your boundless grace toward me leaves me breathless with joy. Amen

---

I held on to him and would not let him go
— Song of Sol. 3:4

If only we would desire God's presence so much that we would cling to Him in our love for His nearness! But mostly we simply wave to Him even in our prayer life because we have other important matters that require our attention. The only exception to this for most of us is when we are in what we perceive to be a critical situation. But all of life is critical.

When will we learn to cling to Him as Jacob did to the angel until he received a blessing? The real blessings of our relationship with God come only to those whose love is such that they are willing to make the extra effort to stay near Him. Though He is always near us, only our responding love can bring forth the richness of that communion.

FATHER, I do need You every hour and You fill my heart with joy because of Your presence. Amen

---

There is no blemish in you — Song of Sol. 4:7

Only twice in any life could such a statement be true of any of us. The first time was when we entered this world as a tiny baby. There was no sin in the heart of that child though some would have imputed the guilt of original sin even to that newborn. None of us can recapture what that innocence was like, but perhaps our search for it is what makes our heart melt watching little children at play. The next time we were without blemish was when we were converted through faith and Jesus washed all our sins away. We might still remember with longing that sense of the newness of everything similar to the newborn child first opening his eyes. Thank God, that does not have to be a distant memory because we can repent of our sin and experience that cleansing and purity again through His forgiveness.

FATHER, make me new again this very hour so that I am fit for this new day. Amen

---

You have made my heart beat faster
— Song of Sol. 4:9

Far too many regular church-goers seldom head to Sunday meetings with anything close to excitement about the services. Most of us may manage some interest in seeing our friends and being involved in some activity while we are there. But when we enter that holy place of worship we don't expect much more than the ordinary procedure we've seen countless times before. We sing, or listen to, the same hymns and choruses. We hear the same people speaking and praying. What is there to get excited about? Perhaps a new song or a new speaker? But if we really determined to meet God there wouldn't that change our attitude and our preparations for worship? What if He really showed up next time?

FATHER, help me keep my eyes open so that I may see You in the midst of all my circumstances today. Amen

---

I opened to my beloved — Song of Sol. 5:6

One of the great aspects of marriage and even of good friendships is that at least with that person we can speak what's on our heart without fear. We have learned that the longer we hold back what we are really thinking the harder it will be to speak the truth later. Those that really love us will allow us to be honest. Why, then, do we try to hold back our true feelings from God? He knows our hearts anyway. It's almost as though if we don't say it then He won't hold it against us. But since God knows our hearts the only one who is harmed by our keeping our feelings toward God to ourselves is ourselves. When we are willing to trust God enough to trust Him with our feelings a whole new realm of joy is opened to us.

FATHER, help me to open myself to the joy of honesty with You. Amen

---

He is wholly desirable — Song of Sol. 5:16

Everyone we have ever known, including close friends, has had his/her flaws. Usually we overlook many of them for that very reason. We, instead, concentrate on the things we have in common and on their attributes that we appreciate. But with our Lord Jesus Christ there are no such limitations. The only thing any of us could ever hold against Him is that in His presence our sin is exposed. On those occasions in the Scriptures when persons rejected Christ it was always because He made them see themselves too clearly. The Bible contains many names for Jesus and many metaphors are used to describe Him. But none of them is adequate to describe the One who is everything to us.

FATHER, teach me to desire You with all my heart so that other longings may not distract me from You. Amen

---

I am my beloved's and my beloved is mine
— Song of Sol. 6:3

Few things are more precious to observe than a young couple recently married who still are so absorbed in their love for each other that nothing else matters. How sad it is to see that devotion get eroded by so many other life concerns! Most of our relationships devolve into a routine that has little of the passion with which it began. All too often the same thing happens with our relationship with our heavenly Father. We know He will always be there for us and, as a result, we often begin to take our relationship for granted. After all we have other matters of concern and He will wait a while. When you actually say that out loud or even read it to yourself as here you can see what a tragic mistake it is. Too often we only recognize this tragedy when we are confronted with some other tragic circumstance of life.

FATHER, help me to learn dependence and commitment without necessity. Amen

---

She is the pure child of the one who bore her
— (Song of Sol. 6:9)

Looking back over your life you may sometimes wonder if you have properly embodied the good attributes of your parents. You may want those who know you best to be able to see those things in you. You may rightly feel some pride if they do. But are those who know you best also able to see a resemblance to Jesus in you? They see you when no one else does. They know you in those private moments when you can be off stage and let your hair down. But, then, because they know and love you they may overlook some of your less admirable qualities. It is also important that we show a family resemblance to the Father in public; not just when we are trying to put on our best face, but also when we are dealing with them in a business or social context. Even in those times, is the Father proud to call you His own?

FATHER, I want to make You proud of me today even when I'm all alone. Amen

———————

[You are] the work of the hands of an artist
— Song of Sol. 7:1

None of us likes to overhear someone berating another person for their performance or their appearance. Such "put-downs" make us all cringe a bit as though we fear our own condemnation coming next. We have been told for a long time now that giving praise and encouragement always brings better results than negative criticism. One positive reminder that each of us needs on a regular basis is that, just as surely as Adam and Eve were formed by the loving hands of the Master Designer, we too were fashioned in His love. The Psalmist surely spoke for each of us in saying that we are fearfully and wonderfully made. When others look down on us we can be encouraged by the knowledge that we are the work of His hands.

FATHER, remind me today that you fashioned my innermost being for fellowship with You. Amen

---

His desire is for me — Song of Sol. 7:10

More and more these days it is easy to get the feeling that you are nothing but a face in the crowd or that you are nothing more than a number to the bureaucracy of government. Or perhaps you feel that to your employer you are nothing but a small cog in a large wheel. Perhaps it is for that reason that so many people, like small children, are acting out just to get someone's attention. But with God there is no anonymity. The Scriptures teach that the Father knows us so well that even the hairs on our head are numbered by Him. And this Creator of the ends of the earth who knows each of us so intimately still loves us without limit. Even more astoundingly, He doesn't just love us all, but loves each one of us with a love willing to give Himself as a sacrifice.

FATHER, I am overwhelmed by the knowledge that You love me without condition and without limit. Amen

———————

Put me like a seal over your heart
— Song of Sol. 8:6

How do you remember the ones you love? There are various external ways such as photographs or other mementos that serve as reminders. But how do you remember God? Here again there are countless things that jog our physical senses to thoughts of God. The Bible shows us, however, that those stimulants to the senses can become the full extent of our thoughts of God. Then our religion becomes nothing more than the trappings. But our Father wants us to recall His love for us in deeper ways. He desires that our thoughts of Him reach to the depths of our soul. Because of His boundless love for us, God stirs the fires of our heart and reminds us that He is always there waiting for us.

FATHER, I am drawn by Your strong love each moment to enjoy continuing fellowship with You. Amen

———————

Hurry, my beloved! — Song of Sol. 8:14

Waiting for anything is difficult whether it is good or bad. If the wait is for something unpleasant that is surely on its way you may feel relief at the delay while, at the same time, feeling heightening anxiety at what it may turn out to be. But waiting for something you have longed for has its downside as well. An awaited event that promises great joy may lose some of its attraction as the interim time drags by. Or our hearts may yearn for its coming so much that we become obsessed to the exclusion of all other concerns. We surely long for the consummation to be ushered in by the return of Christ in power. But that desire must not blind us to the countless throng for whom His return will bring condemnation.

FATHER, I long for the time of Your coming, but I also pray for more time for the lost to come home. Amen

---

Printed in the United States
122696LV00001B/43-111/P